THE NIGHT HUNTER'S PREY

By the same author:
SOLDIER OF THE RAJ
ADMIRAL OF THE BLUE
BLOODLINE
LIFELINE

IAIN GORDON

The
Night Hunter's
Prey

The Lives and Deaths of
an RAF Rear Gunner and a
Luftwaffe Pilot

Pen & Sword
AVIATION

First published in Great Britain in 2016 by
PEN & SWORD AVIATION
An imprint of
Pen & Sword Books Ltd
47 Church Street
Barnsley
South Yorkshire, S70 2AS

Copyright © Iain Gordon, 2016

ISBN 978 1 47388 250 8

Printed and bound in England by
CPI Group (UK) Ltd, Croydon, CR0 4YY

Pen & Sword Books Ltd incorporates the imprints of Aviation, Atlas,
Family History, Fiction, Maritime, Military, Discovery, Politics,
History, Archaeology, Select, Wharncliffe Local History, Wharncliffe
True Crime, Military Classics, Wharncliffe Transport, Leo Cooper,
The Praetorian Press, Remember When, Seaforth Publishing and
Frontline Publishing.

For a complete list of Pen & Sword titles please contact
PEN & SWORD BOOKS LIMITED
47 Church Street, Barnsley, South Yorkshire, S70 2AS, England
E-mail: enquiries@pen-and-sword.co.uk
Website: www.pen-and-sword.co.uk

Contents

List of Illustrations

EQUIVALENT SERVICE RANKS AND ROYAL AIR FORCE ABBREVIATIONS

COMMISSIONED OFFICERS

Royal Navy	Army	Royal Air Force	
Admiral of the Fleet	Field Marshal	Marshal of the Royal Air Force	MRAF
Admiral	General	Air Chief Marshal	Air Chf Mshl
Vice Admiral	Lieutenant General	Air Marshal	Air Mshl
Rear Admiral	Major General	Air Vice Marshal	AVM
Commodore	Brigadier	Air Commodore	Air Cdre
Captain	Colonel	Group Captain	Gp Capt
Commander	Lieutenant Colonel	Wing Commander	Wg Cdr
Lieutenant Commander	Major	Squadron Leader	Sqn Ldr
Lieutenant	Captain	Flight Lieutenant	Flt Lt
Sub Lieutenant	Lieutenant	Flying Officer	Fg Off
Midshipman	Second Lieutenant	Pilot Officer	Plt Off

NON-COMMISSIONED OFFICERS

Royal Navy	Army	Royal Air Force	
Warrant Officer	Warrant Officer	Warrant Officer	WO
Chief Petty Officer	Sergeant Major	Flight Sergeant	Flt Sgt
Petty Officer	Sergeant	Sergeant	Sgt

OTHER RANKS

Royal Navy	Army	Royal Air Force	
Leading Seaman	Corporal	Leading Aircraftman	LAC
Able Seaman	Lance Corporal	Aircraftman Class 1	AC1
Ordinary Seaman	Private	Aircraftman Class 2	AC2

Prologue

For anyone who lived near a Bomber Command airfield during the Second World War the memories will never fade: the ululating roar in the middle of the day, rising to a crescendo then fading to a low, purposeful drone as mighty engines were run up and tested – the engines which would later drag the great, heavily-laden bombers off the concrete runways and carry them across the North Sea to engage the enemy and, with luck, bring them safely back again.

After dusk came the nightly takeoff ritual; successive waves of sound as one after another the bombers roared down the runway with throttles fully open; then the great dark shapes passed overhead in their sinister cavalcade, one every few minutes, the passage of the whole force sometimes lasting for over an hour. Then, when it seemed the show was over, there came the distant sound of more aircraft from other stations as they struggled to gain height and join the bomber stream until one was surrounded by the reverberating drone of bombers on their way to war. If the operation was a major one and the night was clear, the sky would seem black with their purposeful forms. At last the great east-bound armada passed out of earshot and sleep became possible.

In the early hours the squadrons started to return – not in the ordered succession in which they had departed but singly or in ragged groups of two or three. Sometimes an aircraft would be flying unusually low or would be making a different sound as it limped home with damaged airframe or with one or more engines out of commission. These casualties usually arrived much later than the others and sometimes a rumbling explosion like thunder and the scream of tearing metal would tell the sad tale of another cripple which had not quite made it home.

The next morning word would spread through the civilian community of those aircraft which had failed to return and of any which had crashed in the vicinity. Children on bicycles or on foot would rush to seek out the latest wreck in field or spinney, its sad body twisted and its tail or a wing pointing grotesquely and unnaturally into the air. Later in the day a huge RAF Scammel recovery vehicle would squeeze its way down narrow country lanes to the place where a row of decapitated trees or a broken down hedgerow and a group of light-blue uniformed guards marked the site of the accident; the great dead monster would be removed leaving the ground scarred forever and strewn with broken perspex and other sad relics for later retrieval by small boys to add to their collections, or as swops. Tragedy was re-enacted nightly but it was wartime and death was more especially a normal part of life.

Aircraft recognition cards and charts with the silhouettes of allied and enemy aircraft were to be found in most public buildings and in the possession of many families and groups. Heaven help any boy who, among his peers, could not tell the difference between a Lancaster and a Halifax, or a Heinkel and a Dornier.

The airfield became the hub of the community. Most of the road traffic in the area was RAF staff cars, ambulances, motorcycles and trucks – Bedfords, Commers and the ubiquitous Chevrolet 15 cwt GP trucks made in Canada to British specifications. The roads resounded with the characteristic hiss of their tyres and whine of their transmission. Many men and women, too young or too old for active service, depended, directly or indirectly, upon the airfield for their employment and most of the local shops relied upon service customers to keep their businesses solvent.

RAF personnel usually outnumbered the local civilians; the 'Erks', or aircraftmen who serviced the planes and their equipment and ran the airfield, were mainly qualified tradesmen and, on balance, probably behaved better in the local pubs than their counterparts in the Army and Navy. But the real stars were the aircrew, the young gods who proudly wore junior officers' rings or sergeants' stripes and the brevets of pilots, observers and air gunners. They filled the pubs and their stentorian badinage and laughter proscribed all attempts at conversation by other customers; but they were held in deep respect and were treated with the amused tolerance and affection which has always been accorded to unruly heroes. The locals soon learned not to enquire about the absence of a particular airman; losses were so regular and so heavy that the unspoken convention among aircrew was to make no mention of them and to restrict mourning to a brief and understated verbal tribute to a lost friend. There could be no other way; life had to carry on and tomorrow it could be themselves.

Memorial to the Canadian crew of a Wellington bomber which crashed in the Brecon Beacons in July 1942. This is one of hundreds of similar memorials throughout Britain to the crews of Allied bombers lost in training or returning from operations.

NIGEL DAVIES

What sort of people were these men? There were a few public school boys and university graduates and undergraduates but by far the greater number of aircrew volunteers were very ordinary young men in very ordinary occupations. Those with a technical training, such as electricians or mechanics, tended to be directed to trades allied to their skills but those without, such as clerks, teachers and salesmen, were ideal material for aircrew. They would be required to handle complicated machines and equipment so a reasonable level of education was required which was then augmented within the service by thorough training courses ranging from nine months for an air gunner to two years for a pilot.

It was a strange form of warfare in which they were engaged: Bomber Command was statistically the most hazardous branch of the Allied armed services, requiring immense courage and endurance, and yet aircrew were able to lead lives nearer to normal than any other servicemen; when their night's work was done, those who returned could enjoy relatively normal life and liberties, sleeping in their own beds, eating normal meals with their friends and enduring none of the round-the-clock privations of the infantryman in the field or the sailor on Atlantic or Arctic convoys.

Their initial tour of duty was for 30 operations; if their aircraft had to turn back due to mechanical problems, it did not count. A strong bond of friendship and trust developed between individual crew members who would often do a few extra operations in order to finish at the same time as a mate. Those who survived would then normally become instructors for about a year before embarking on their second tour. Their chances of surviving the first tour were about one in six; and the second tour one in forty. In a group of 100 bomber crewmen 55 would be killed in action, 18 wounded or shot down leaving only 27 who would survive the war physically unscathed. Mental damage was another matter: those who simply could not take the pressure and broke down, or requested a release from operations, were stripped of their rank and their brevet and branded as LMF, Lacking Moral Fibre, a condemnation which would follow them for the rest of their service lives.

The first time that many of the locals in the towns and villages in the East of England had heard foreign accents was when the bomber stations were established and the British airmen were joined by Canadians, Australians, New Zealanders and a few Americans who were not prepared to wait until the USA entered the war. Their numbers increased steadily as the war progressed and they were joined by South Africans, Rhodesians, Caribbeans, Poles, Czechs and Free French. Some 20,000 Australians and 50,000 Canadians served in Bomber Command either integrated with British crews or in their own RAAF and RCAF squadrons. Canada even had its own Group, No.6 (Canadian) Group, comprising up to 14 squadrons.

With the arrival of the US Army Air Force in 1942, the East of England acquired yet another level of national diversity. The American 8th Air Force took over 41 bomber airfields in the East of England and around

350,000 US servicemen served in these stations during the war. Local men and women who had never been further than their county market town suddenly found themselves surrounded by these friendly people who spoke an unfamiliar form of English and spent more money than they had ever imagined was in circulation; and it was the first time that most of them had ever seen a black man, or someone chewing gum. The Allied bomber force and its enormous support organisation had taken over vast tracts of East Anglia, Lincolnshire and Yorkshire which had become more cosmopolitan than London or Paris; their presence became the sole topic of conversation in the shops and memories of the old rural ways gradually faded as this new society, dominated by men of war from far off lands, became the norm.

The other abiding memory of childhood in wartime England was the bomber traffic coming the other way: the rising and falling note of the air raid siren then the throbbing drone of the approaching German bombers – a sound unlike any other; the dash for the air raid shelter in 'siren suit' or for sanctuary under the staircase or kitchen table from where one would listen to the crash and rumble of enemy bombs and the steady thump from our own ack-ack batteries until the continuous note of the all-clear was heard. To a child, these nights held no terror; to be dragged from bed and rushed to a shelter was simply an exciting game and the louder the bangs the better the experience. The child had no conception of the anxiety and distress suffered by the adults in the family. Next morning there would be dust in the air, rubble at the roadside where houses once stood and strands of silver foil in the fields and hedgerows.

Sometimes one of the raiders would be brought down relatively intact; it might be put on triumphal display for a few days before the RAF would take it away for examination and trial. The more serious enemy crashes were a priority target for souvenir hunters; a strip of canvas with a swastika or German cross was the ultimate prize but many houses treasured instruments, tally plates and engine parts.

Later in the war one became used to the unmistakeable rasping growl of the V1 'Doodlebug' and the silence as everyone waited for the engine to cut, the delay before the mighty explosion and the speculation as to where it had fallen which followed. They were the sights and sounds of the bomber war, once seen and heard never to be forgotten.

After the war the Allied legions were repatriated and the towns and villages slowly returned to austere normality as the bomber airfields were decommissioned, their runways and dispersals dug up and returned to farmland or lying silent and sinister awaiting some form of development. Today those that were not restored for agriculture are mainly covered by housing or industrial estates; the occasional control tower or hangar is preserved and odd lengths of runway to remind the visitor that this was once a bustling military airfield which never slept.

On a quiet summer's evening when the activity of the day has subsided, it is still possible, for those who knew them in their heyday, to stand awhile in such places and recall the roar of the bombers as they thundered down the runway; and in the pubs around the old airfields to remember the animated discourse of those extraordinary young men most of whom lost their lives and are commemorated on the memorials in their home towns and villages, but whose ghosts must surely still inhabit these deserted and melancholy places.

MINISTRY OF INFORMATION PHOTOGRAPH TAKEN BY CECIL BEATON 1941

Pilot and Co-Pilot of a Wellington Bomber.

Chapter 1 – "One of the boys"

R.A.F. Marham, Norfolk, 1800 hrs, 27th November 1940

The whine of the starboard engine turning over was broken by a sharp report as it fired and spluttered into faltering life. The pilot released the starter button keeping his finger on the adjacent booster coil button until the engine had picked up and settled down to a steady beat. The ground crew beneath the engine, their coats ballooning in the slipstream, screwed down the priming pump, turned the priming cock to off and closed the engine cowling door. The pilot slowly opened the throttle until the engine reached its warming up speed of 1,000 rpm. The procedure was repeated for the port engine.

As the aircraft stood on its dispersal with both engines warming up, the pilot began his engine and installation tests. Temperatures and pressures were observed and the flaps were raised and lowered to check the hydraulic system. When the oil pressure of each engine had reached 15°C and the cylinder temperature 120°C, he increased speed to 1,500 rpm for a precautionary check of each magneto. While still at 1,500 rpm he changed each engine to high gear observing the momentary drop in oil pressure and ensuring that it returned to normal after a few seconds. Changing back to low gear he opened both engines up further to 2,400 rpm before checking the operation of the constant speed propeller. With the propeller controls right forward he then fully opened each throttle control to check take-off boost and static rpm.

Dust from the dispersal blasted across the airfield in the increased slipstream and the roar of the two huge Bristol Pegasus engines could be heard in the surrounding fields and villages for miles around. The pilot prepared to move off and undertook his final checks before getting under way: Brake Pressure – at least 120 lbs/sq ins; Hatches closed; Fuel Levels OK; Pressure Head Heater – ON. He eased the throttles open together, released the brakes and the bomber started rolling ahead towards the junction with the perimeter track.

Once on the perimeter track, the pilot increased speed to start the long taxi to the head of the runway. His aircraft, 'A-Able' T 2520, was to take off first with 'E-Easy' T 2560 close behind. A total of eleven aircraft from the squadron were to take off on operations that night but with different targets so those with the longest flight would take off earliest. Some were only heading for Boulogne, just across the Channel, but 'A-Able' was bound for Cologne in the enemy's heartland. At the head of the runway the pilot stopped the aircraft, turned into the direction of take-off and, with the assistance of his second pilot, began the final pre-take-off checks – Trimming Tabs and Flaps, Mixture and Propeller controls. At last the aircraft was ready for take-off.

A green light flashed and 'A-Able' was cleared for take-off. The pilot eased both throttles up to full power and the aircraft started its high-speed journey down the runway; both throttles were held fully open to avoid even the smallest loss of power. As the speed increased the tail lifted and the aircraft started to pull heavily to starboard like a headstrong horse. The pilot, with long experience of Wellington bombers, knew this tendency well – particularly with a heavy bomb load. 'A-Able' was fully loaded with four 500 lb and six 250 lb general-purpose, high-explosive bombs plus a parcel of incendiaries and the pilot had opened the starboard throttle slightly ahead of the port throttle to counteract the swing he knew this load would cause; he now used the rudder to keep the aircraft straight on its course. The two great engines strained to the limit of their combined 2,100 horse power in their resolve to lift the heavily laden bomber off the ground; the fuselage flexed and the aircraft vibrated at every loose component in its frenetic endeavour; 75 mph, 85 mph and the end of the runway was approaching fast. At a ground speed of just over 100 mph the pilot eased his control column back and lifted the aircraft gently off the ground. The undercarriage cleared the perimeter fence by some 10 feet. As 'A-Able' lifted off 'E-Easy' began its take-off run behind.

On an order from the pilot the second pilot retracted the undercarriage and when the aircraft had reached a safe height of 500 ft the pilot raised the flaps and throttled back to commence the long climb to their operational height. Down below in the villages of Castle Acre and West Lexham farm workers returning home looked up at the drone of the bombers approach, said a silent prayer for the young men who were heading over the North Sea for a brutal confrontation with the enemy and thanked God that they, themselves, were returning to a cosy hearth and a hot meal.

Squadron Leader Norman George Mulholland, the pilot and captain of the aircraft, was an Australian who had started life as a jackeroo at Colombo Station, Charleville, in Queensland.

BASSANO © NATIONAL PORTRAIT GALLERY, LONDON NPGx85366

Wing Commander Norman George Mulholland DFC killed in action 16th February 1942, 458 (Royal Australian Air Force) Squadron.

His father, a skin and wool buyer in Brisbane, died when Norman was 17; the family lost everything and Norman became the principal breadwinner until, ultimately, his mother was remarried to a French farmer near Helensburgh, New South Wales and became Mrs Calvignac. Norman had learnt to fly at the Queensland Aero Club and in 1932 joined the RAF on a short service commission. After four years he left the service and became a pilot with Imperial Airways returning to the RAF on the outbreak of war. This trip to Cologne was his 23rd operation.

With the aircraft settled on a course for a point on the Dutch coast, given to him by the navigator Sergeant Symons, the pilot pushed the intercom button on the right hand side of his control column and addressed his crew:

"Everyone OK? Are you OK back there in the tail Jock?"

"Yes, OK skipper" Sergeant Ollar the rear gunner replied.

The navigator and the wireless operator exchanged a smile and a wink; it was one of the crew's favourite jokes that the captain, with his thick

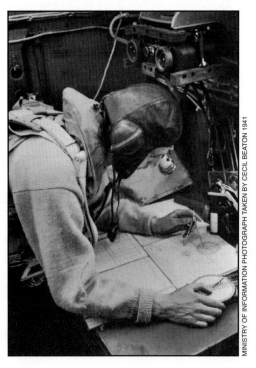

Australian accent, and the Scottish members of the crew could hardly understand a word of what the other was saying. One by one he spoke to each crewman in turn and obtained a positive response – Sergeant Ollar the tail gunner, Sergeant Sutherland the forward gunner, Sergeant Williamson the wireless operator and Sergeant Symons the navigator. Sergeant John Bernard Molony, the second pilot, had been beside him since take-off so needed no such enquiry. Malony was

MINISTRY OF INFORMATION PHOTOGRAPH TAKEN BY CECIL BEATON 1941

Navigator in a Wellington Bomber.

Rear Gunner in a Wellington Bomber. *Note: The turret is turned 90° to the fore and aft line theoretically allowing the gunner to fall backwards through the rear doors to escape in an emergency.*

AUSTRALIAN OFFICIAL PHOTOGRAPHER D. MOGG

perhaps the most well connected of the crew members: he was the son of the Rt Hon Sir Thomas Malony Bart, Vice-Chancellor of the University of Dublin and former Lord Chief Justice of Ireland. On Sir Thomas's retirement the family had moved to Wimbledon, a suburb of London.

Once the aircraft was over the North Sea both gunners came through to the captain on the intercom for permission to test their guns. The rear and front turrets were equipped with twin Browning Mk 11 .303 ins, short-recoil, belt-fed machine guns and there were a further two in the beam positions on either side of the fuselage. The front and rear turrets were power traversing through 180 degrees and were manufactured by a firm whose pre-war experience in the manufacture of the beautifully engineered Fraser-Nash sports cars qualified them well for the design and development of this important aircraft component.

Sergeant Ollar, whose turret had been locked in the fore and aft position during take-off, now unlocked it and tested its traverse to starboard and to port. Having obtained the captain's permission, he then released the safety and fired two short bursts to check that the breech mechanisms were clear and the ammunition belts feeding in correctly. The aircraft shook violently as the guns made themselves heard above the continuous roar of the engines. Ollar reported back to the captain that his turret and guns were in good order and the same procedure was undertaken by Sergeant Sutherland in the forward turret. The worth of a rear gunner could be measured not simply by his skill and accuracy with the guns but by his ability to remain completely alert and vigilant for the full duration of the operation. This could be up to eight or nine hours during which the gunner would be constantly scanning the night skies for the first sign of an enemy fighter. If sighted and preparing to attack, he would call to the pilot for immediate evasive action and the aircraft would dive, corkscrew, wriggle and twist in order to out-manoeuvre its attacker. This, more often than not, proved successful but its success was entirely dependent in the first place on the vigilance and speed of the rear gunner in instigating evasive action. Sergeant Ollar was even more experienced than the captain; this was his 30th operation and he had already shot down two enemy nightfighters.

'A-Able' continued on its journey across the North Sea. At this point in the war a high degree of discretion was given to the captain of each aircraft – he could decide when he would leave, which route he would take and at what height he would fly. Bombers of the same squadron did not fly together in formation and it was not unusual for an aircraft to complete its entire sortie without seeing another plane; but nor was it unusual for mid-air collisions to occur; in cloud and poor visibility when the bomber force was heavy, another aircraft could suddenly appear above or below necessitating violent evasive action. Such action, however, in crowded skies, could then create another potential collision situation at another level. There was also a risk of one aircraft disgorging its bombs on another one below it or, indeed, of receiving the load of the aircraft above. Vigilance was essential for survival.

"Enemy coast ahead" the captain announced over the intercom. They would cross the Dutch coast roughly at the point where the Rivers Meuse, Rhine and Scheldt flow into the sea and the port of Rotterdam gives access to the arterial canal systems of Europe. It was here, six months earlier on 14th May 1940, that Germany had laid the ground rules for area bombing involving heavy civilian casualties when 90 bombers of *Kampfgeschwader 54* dropped 100 tons of bombs on the centre of Rotterdam killing nearly 900 civilians and rendering 85,000 homeless. The attack had been deliberately targeted on civil rather than military or industrial areas with the express purpose of breaking morale and about one square mile of the city centre had been flattened. Later, when British bombing resulted in similar casualties, the indignant Germans were to coin the phrase 'Terror Bombing'.

U.S. NATIONAL ARCHIVES AND RECORDS ADMINISTRATION

S-3134-1

Ruins of the City Centre of Rotterdam after the German raid of 14th May 1940 which killed 900 inhabitants and rendered 85,000 homeless.

As 'A-Able' crossed the coast, searchlight fingers probed the night sky in search of them and showers of anti-aircraft fire, 'flak', reached up for them looking, from the air, like a huge fireworks display. Occasionally a shell burst close to them and the aircraft leapt like a startled deer with the sudden change of pressure. The Wellington bomber could take a lot of punishment that would destroy lesser aircraft. It was designed in the 1930s by Barnes Wallis (of later 'bouncing bomb' renown) using a geodetic airframe of lattice-work duralumin spars. Each section was self supporting making the aircraft extremely strong and often capable of remaining in the air despite serious damage. Wooden battens were attached to the alloy frame to which a linen skin was attached which was then stretched and hardened with several coats of dope. These battens and the lattice-work frame could be seen through the fabric skin which was sometimes burned off during combat exposing the geodetic airframe which, in many cases, maintained its integrity until the aircraft reached home.

Once past the coastal flak, Sergeant Symons, the navigator, gave the captain a course adjustment to bring them to the target. Rotterdam was roughly the halfway point of their journey and from hereon the danger of interception was greatly increased.

"Keep a sharp lookout boys" the captain unnecessarily enjoined his crew over the intercom; they were now on maximum alert without being told. The remaining 75 minutes to the target would pass very slowly.

Target location and bombing accuracy in the early days of the war were very far from exact sciences. With no radar and no dependable means of navigation other than direct reckoning and star sights when visibility permitted, night bombers, more often than not, had no alternative but to drop their loads in the general area where they believed the target to be or to face the hazardous business of returning home with their bombs. If these impediments were then intensified by poor visibility the chances of locating the target were reduced to zero. If the target was correctly identified, the business of hitting it with the bomb load was equally haphazard, depending to a large extent on the nerve of the pilot in holding his course despite the very heavy defensive fire which could be expected around any important installation on the ground. The pilot was guided to the dropping point by instructions from his bomb aimer who lay on his stomach in the nose of the aircraft using a bomb sight which was essentially unchanged since the First World War, the effectiveness of which depended largely upon an accurate input of wind direction and speed which, in itself, was difficult to establish with certainty.

Cologne was a large city each district of which looked much the same as the next from the air; but it had one great advantage – it was built on a major river, the Rhine, which, if it could be sighted and its bends and bridges identified, would be of great value to 'A-Able' in locating the railway marshalling yards which were its target. In April 1910 the City of Cologne had completed a major railway engineering project known as the *Güterumgehungsbahn Köln*. This was a bypass of the city for rail freight traffic, thereby avoiding the busy central passenger station and connecting the huge marshalling yards to the north and south of the city with those on the east bank of the Rhine. The bypass line crossed the river by the *Südbrücke*, South Bridge, a dedicated two-track rail bridge of distinctive three-tied-arch design. If this bridge could be identified it would show a clear path to the marshalling yards.

A further slight course adjustment to port brought 'A-Able' heading direct for the city centre which the navigator reckoned they would reach in about twelve minutes. To the captain's surprise and puzzlement there was no barrage of flak to welcome them as would normally be expected.

Sergeant Symons, who was also a trained bomb aimer, was already in position in the nose straining his eyes for any recognisable feature. At the briefing before take-off he had been given a map of the target area. During the flight Sergeant Molony, the second pilot, had flown the aircraft while Symons and the captain had studied this map in detail; they both knew exactly what they were looking for.

"There's the river Skip" Symons reported excitedly, "about ten degrees to starboard; come a bit right."

"Well done" Mulholland replied as he turned the aircraft as directed, "look out for bridges, any bridges."

As 'A-Able' approached the river both airmen recognised a bend in its course from the map they had been studying which told them they were approaching the northern region of the city. All they had to do now was to follow the river upstream, past the city centre, until they identified the South Bridge that would lead them to the marshalling yards.

"There Skipper, turn right" Symons called and the captain turned the aircraft 90 degrees to starboard until they were following the course of the river. A few minutes later Sergeant Symons reported to the captain that he could see a suspension bridge with other bridges further on.

"The first must be the *Mülheimer* so we're getting close." The next bridge had three arches.

"That looks just like the *Südbrücke*" the captain said.

"No. Look. Isn't that the cathedral on the west bank? That's more or less level with the *Hohenzollernbrücke* according to the map." Even at night and from the air the twin spires of this ancient gothic monument, one of the largest churches in Europe, could be identified at the west end of the bridge.

"You're right. So the next one is the *Hindenburg* and our boy must be the one after that" the captain replied as he altered course slightly to starboard.

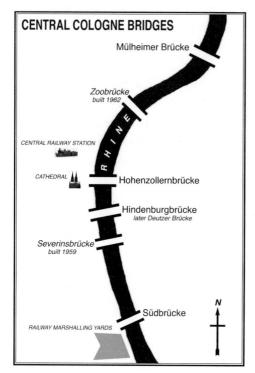

CENTRAL COLOGNE BRIDGES

Mülheimer Brücke

Zoobrücke
built 1962

RHINE

CENTRAL RAILWAY STATION

CATHEDRAL

Hohenzollernbrücke

Hindenburgbrücke
later Deutzer Brücke

Severinsbrücke
built 1959

Südbrücke

N

RAILWAY MARSHALLING YARDS

Minutes later Symons recognised the three distinctive arches of the *Südbrücke*. "Got it Skip. Looks like the Forth Bridge".

The second pilot, pointed through the perspex of the cockpit windscreen: "There are the marshalling yards; over there on the west bank."

A thin black line which was the railway track could be seen leading from the bridge to a vast, dense area which was the southern marshalling yards – their target.

"Have you got it now?" Mulholland asked the bomb aimer, "Over to starboard?"

"Yes, got it Skip."

"Take us in then," the captain said as he altered course towards the yards. From hereon the aircraft was in the hands of Sergeant Symons whose instructions he would follow to the letter. Everything they had seen on the ground so far had been observed through breaks in heavy cloud. They had been extremely lucky in recognising the bend in the river and the *Südbrücke* and now could only hope that their good fortune would hold until they had dropped their bombs.

In the early days of bombing in World War 1, aircraft had to fly along the line of the wind to counteract drift to left or right. This was a dangerous restriction as it enabled the anti-aircraft batteries on the ground to site their guns on the line of the prevailing wind thereby greatly increasing their chance of success. This was overcome with the invention of the Course Setting Bomb Sight or 'Wimperis Sight' after its inventor, Harry Wimperis, an aeronautical engineer who was Director of Scientific Research at the Air Ministry. The sight had a built-in compass on which the aimer entered the wind direction; then with three separate knobs he would enter windspeed, airspeed and altitude. The most problematic of these was the wind direction which the aimer could calculate in a variety of different ways all of which involved the pilot changing course in various directions during the approach to the target. Once entered, the sight would calculate the angle of drift and indicate the course on which the aircraft must fly to pass directly over the target. Wellington bombers in 1940 were mainly fitted with the Mark VII Wimperis sight which, though still fairly crude and lacking the stability which a gyroscope would later bring to bombsights, were a great improvement over the earlier generation.

With the data entered into his sight and the aircraft flying on the indicated course Sergeant Symons lay on his stomach watching the target through the perspex window in the fuselage as it got gradually closer.

"Right a bit Skip. Steady there." He and the captain had flown on many missions together and had established an excellent rapport for this final, vital approach to the target; each man knew exactly how the other would react.

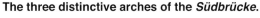

The three distinctive arches of the *Südbrücke*.

A. SAVIN

"Right a bit; a bit more; OK steady." In his right hand Symons held a device like an old bell pull with a button at the end over which his thumb was poised and ready. The marshalling yards were now clearly visible through a break in the cloud; the centre of the target was coming into his sight.

"Right a fraction Skip; spot on." his thumb closed on the button and the aircraft shuddered with new found levity as the great load of destruction dropped from its belly.

"Bombs away" he announced.

"Big explosions and smoke below Skipper" Sergeant Ollar soon reported from his vantage point in the rear turret.

So intent had the crew been in pinpointing and striking the target that they had almost forgotten the uncanny lack of anti-aircraft fire. Then, suddenly, there was a blinding flash as fourteen or fifteen searchlights switched on in unison turning the sky above the city centre into a vast floodlit stage which they were just entering from the wings. The captain banked steeply in an attempt to get out of the deadly illumination; he knew that if they got caught in the cone of the searchlights no amount of wriggling would get them out of it and they would be a sitting duck for the anti-aircraft guns below. As he pulled the aircraft out of the searchlights' glare he knew this would not be the end of it; they had been observed by the gun crews who would be determined to prevent their escape. Sure enough a crash like thunder shook the aircraft violently as the first shell exploded some way below them; it was only a matter of time before the gunners got their range. The searchlights had now broken formation and were probing the sky individually.

In the rear turret Sergeant Ollar had been watching their antics until, suddenly, the beams locked together again and he could see another bomber far astern of them caught in the lethal cone.

"Skip" he called over the internet, "they've got some other poor bugger pinned down astern of us. Looks like another Wimpy." This was the universally-used nickname for the Wellington bomber.

"Keep an eye on him Jock." Now that the attention of the searchlights had been diverted, for the time being at least, they must now get back on a course to get them away from Cologne and back towards the coast.

Wellington Mk.1 Bombers of 75 (NZ) Squadron in November 1940.

A single searchlight probing the sky ahead of them caught their port wing as it passed and immediately swung back illuminating the whole aircraft. Squadron Leader Mulholland began to zigzag fiercely and when out of the glare for a moment banked steeply to starboard. The searchlight's beam swept back and forth in search of them until it gave up and joined the others which were floodlighting the sky above the city centre.

As 'A-Able' hurried from the scene Sergeant Ollar watched the firework display through his turret's perspex which had been polished by the ground crew before take-off until there was not a single mark or smear on it which might impede the gunner's vision in any way or distract attention from his ceaseless search of the sky.

"All hell's been let loose back there Skipper" he reported, "and there's a lot of fires and smoke on the ground in different areas but our target looks the brightest and best."

The Captain smiled to himself with satisfaction and hoped that the camera in the aircraft's belly had obtained a good shot of the blazing marshalling yards for the staff officers who would examine them minutely in due course. Tomorrow perhaps, or the next day, another bomber over Cologne would take another photograph which would show more clearly exactly how much damage had been done; and so intelligence was accumulated, the effectiveness of raids assessed and future raids planned.

Though 'A-Able' was now on its way home, vigilance could not be relaxed for a moment. Four months earlier in July 1940 *Reichsmarschall* Hermann Göring, Commander-in-Chief of the *Luftwaffe* (German air force), had decreed that a *Nachtjagd* (nightfighter force) should be trained and established on airfields in Holland to guard Germany's western approaches from the ever increasing bombing raids from England. The aircraft of the *Nachtjagd,* specially equipped and adapted for hunting in darkness and supported by *Freya,* a ground based radar which warned them of approaching British aircraft, were just as great a hazard to homeward bound bombers as those on their way to Germany.

As they approached the Dutch coast Ollar saw two indistinct shapes some distance astern of them. As they passed slowly from left to right they banked and he could see from their silhouettes that they were twin engined aircraft but he could not identify their type. They might have been Messerschmitt bf110s or Junkers Ju88s both of which were used by the *Luftwaffe* as nightfighters. He reported them to the captain and watched them carefully as they disappeared from view. They obviously had not seen them or had been after something else. They did not reappear.

Once over the sea Sergeant Symons, now back at his navigating table, gave the captain a new course for home. Though remaining ever watchful, the danger of nightfighters was always present until they were safely home, the extreme tension of the past four hours was now relaxed a little and chocolate rations and thermos flasks of coffee came out for some well earned refreshment. The temperature during the operation had dropped to minus 20°C in places and despite thick clothing and fur lined boots the men were chilled to the bone. At the height of the action they had been too focussed on their duties to notice how cold they were but now, as they approached home, they became aware of it. The hot coffee helped.

At 2315 the captain started his approach run to Marham and could see that although there was still a lot of cloud, visibility for landing should not be a problem. He reduced speed to 140 mph and, assisted by Sergeant Molony, began his pre-landing checks: Brake Pressure – not less than 100 lbs/sq.ins.; Carburettor Air Intakes – Cold; Gills – Closed; Elevator Trimming Tabs – Neutral. The runway was clear ahead. Mixture Controls – Normal; Propeller Controls – Levers Fully Forward. On the captain's order Molony lowered the undercarriage with the selector lever above the compass; there was a thump as it locked into position; the indicator light and an audible signal, which he had tested earlier, confirmed that it was engaged correctly. Speed was now down to 85 mph as the aircraft passed over the perimeter fence; a bump as the wheels touched the runway, a reduction in engine speed and 'A-Able' was home. The time was 2335, they had been airborne for 5 hours and 5 minutes.

When the aircraft had come to a standstill the captain raised the flaps with the lever next to the undercarriage selector and Molony opened the cowling gills with the two little handles below the flying instrument panel. As they taxied towards the dispersal the crew could see three large staff cars and a group of senior officers beside them. It was unusual to have a reception committee and Mulholland wondered what was going on. When they reached their dispersal he turned the aircraft into the wind and ran the engines at 800 rpm to cool them. He then opened up gradually and evenly and ran at –2 lbs/sq ins boost for 5 seconds, then throttled back to 800 rpm and ran for 2 minutes before throttling right back and pulling the slow-running cutout controls to stop the engines. Molony switched off the ignition and turned off all fuel cocks.

With the continuous roar of the engines in their ears for the past five hours, the sudden silence seemed unnatural to the crew members who still felt a humming in their ears as they collected their kit and scrambled through the fuselage to the exit hatch. As they dropped one by one onto the tarmac, the staff cars were explained: to their astonishment, at the head of a group of very senior officers was the most senior of them all – His Majesty King George VI.

The King shook hands with each crew member as he emerged from the fuselage and had a cheerful word for every one. He smiled when he saw

KING SPENDS NIGHT WITH BOMBERS

ort direct from Cologne raid

'Make two runs over the target'

HM The King (extreme left) with crew members at a bomber station "somewhere in England".

painted on the nose of the bomber a flying kangaroo with a 'Joey' in its pouch and a boomerang below. The Australian captain told him that the boomerang had brought them all safely back after many hazardous missions. Though it was well below freezing on the airfield, the King excused himself so he could go and meet another aircraft coming in and told them he would see them again at the debriefing.

Later, having had a mug of beef tea with the airmen, he asked them about their mission.

"Were you able to drop your bombs on the target" he asked.

"Yes Sir. The weather wasn't good and we had nine-tenths cloud." Mulholland replied, "but I managed to pick up a bend in the Rhine which gave me my direction."

"Was there much opposition?" the King asked.

"Well Sir, Jerry is still playing foxy. There were no searchlights, no flak, until I dropped my bombs. Then fourteen or fifteen lights came on making a cone in the sky and Jerry chucked everything up from their AA guns to the apex of the cone." When the King was told that Squadron Leader Mulholland had made twenty-three flights over Germany he asked him:

"Have you been to Berlin?"

"Oh yes Sir" replied Mulholland, "I know that place quite well."

The King chatted with every member of the crew for quite some time before adjourning to the Sergeants' Mess for a stiff whisky and soda. He had dined in the Officers' Mess while 'A-Able' was over Germany. They were later told how the King had been in the operations room when one of the pilots in the air forgot to turn off his microphone and shouted at his talkative wireless operator to "shut the f**k up." The King had laughed as heartily as everyone else – he had served in the Royal Navy and was not easily shocked!

The story as it apeared in *The Australian Women's Weekly*
of 14th December 1940.

KING'S TALK WITH SYDNEY AIRMEN

Norman Mulholland found him "like one of the boys"

By Brian Wickham from MARY ST. CLAIRE, Our London Representative.

When Australian Squadron Leader Norman George Mulholland stepped down from his Wellington bomber before dawn after his twenty-third raid on Germany, the first man he met at the R.A.F. station was the King.

Sergeant Ollar wrote to his wife:

"He laughed and joked with us just as if he was a member of the crew. He wanted to hear all the ins and outs of our daily lives and our duties on operations. Knowing I was a Scot and a gunner, he told me that his shooting holidays at Balmoral were among his favourite times. As he left, he waved across the room to me and said 'Good shooting!'"

The Squadron Leader summed it up in an interview with Mary St. Claire, London Correspondent of *The Australian Women's Weekly:* "We were all completely relaxed. He was just like one of the boys."

THE RUINS OF COLOGNE IN 1945.

The *Hohenzollernbrücke* withstood continuous aerial attacks throughout the war and was finally demolished by German Army Engineers in 1945 as the Allied advance approached the city. Its remains can be seen above in line with the great cathedral which also withstood considerable punishment.

Closer to the camera is the wreckage of the Hindenburgbrucke, now known as the *Deutzer Brücke*, which collapsed in 1945 during restoration work and was later rebuilt.

The *Mülheimer Brücke* (not visible) was destroyed in a raid by the USAAF in October 1944.

The *Sudbrücke* (not visible) was destroyed by Allied bombing in January 1945.

The *Severinsbrücke* (1959) and the *Zoobrücke* (1962) were added to the Cologne Rhine crossings as the city's postwar rail and road traffic developed.

Alec aged about twelve.

SS *City of York* **in the Suez Canal.**

Chapter 2 – Early Days

Alexander Johnston Stewart Ollar was born on 3rd December 1910 in Calcutta where his father, an engineer, was the government Chief Inspector of Factories. On the outbreak of war in 1914 his parents decided that he and his sister Mary, who was three years older than him, should be sent to their paternal grandparents in Scotland for the duration of the war.

So it was that Alexander, aged four, had his first glimpse of the UK as he, together with his mother and sister, disembarked from the SS *City of York* at Tilbury on 26th May 1915. It had been a long voyage stopping at Madras, Colombo, Port Said and, finally Marseilles. In peacetime, the very affluent passengers would have disembarked here taking the *Blue Train* to Paris, then on to the Channel Ports for a short sea crossing instead of the long, and often stormy, haul around Gibraltar and across the Bay of Biscay. However, this was wartime and the French railway system was in turmoil with priority naturally being given to military traffic.

A taxi took the family to Euston Station in Central London from where they caught the London, Midland and Scottish overnight express to Glasgow. Arriving at Glasgow Central in the early hours, the children professed themselves to be starving and all their mother could obtain on the station were brawn sandwiches made, they later learnt, from every unmentionable part of an animal which could not be sold in its unminced form. This, after the exotic Indian food prepared by their own cook to which they were accustomed, was far from agreeable but at least it staved off the pangs of hunger.

From Glasgow Central Station they were directed to Glasgow Bridge Wharf where they boarded the TS *Queen Alexandra* which would take them to Campbeltown at the foot of the Kintyre peninsula. As the ship made its way down the Clyde past docks with ships from every corner of the world, and busy shipyards building vessels which would sail to every corner of the world, the industrial waterfront gradually gave way to the green fields and rolling hills of the Clyde Estuary. This was the classic route that Glaswegians took for their holidays 'doon the watter' to Wemyss Bay and Rothesay on the Isle of Bute. From here the steamer continued to Largs, Lochranza on the north coast of Arran and then the long leg down the Kilbrannan Sound to Campbeltown.

Had the children known in which direction to look, as the *Queen Alexandra* entered Campbeltown Loch, they would have seen their grandparents' house, just above the shoreline directly ahead. Instead, their attention was focussed on the small crowd waiting on the quayside to meet passengers off the ship. Their uncle, Alexander, had no difficult in recognising them as they crossed the gangway and hastened to welcome them and conduct them to a waiting horse and trap; their luggage followed on separately with a local carrier.

The Ollar household at Kilkerran comprised Alec's grandparents, three unmarried aunts – Minnie, Kate and Martha and one unmarried uncle, Alexander, who had met them at the quay. This meant there were now three Alexanders in the house; the grandfather had always been known as Sandy and to differentiate between the two Alecs they became Alec *Mhor*, Big Alec, and Alec *Beg*, Wee Alec and so he would always be known in the family, even when he was six foot tall!

Sandy Ollar, their grandfather, had as a boy been destined to follow a family tradition and study medicine until one summer when he was staying with an uncle in Carradale and was helping out in the fields during the harvest. An accident with the reaper left his arm badly mangled and his uncle, the local doctor, had no choice but to amputate his nephew's arm. Doctor Johnston had been a naval surgeon for much of his career, at one time having served on Queen Victoria's Royal Yacht, and was very experienced with amputations in difficult conditions. He made a clean job of it and there were no complications.

With medicine no longer an option, young Sandy had then devoted himself to amateur horticulture and the breeding of show poultry. He became a famous grower of pansies and breeder of exotic chickens winning every show in the west of Scotland, year after year. It is said that a letter from Holland addressed to: 'The Pansy King, Scotland' was delivered to him without difficulty or delay. This, of course, was in the days before the title might have had rather different connotations.

Alec and his sister Mary with their grandfather at Kilkerran.

The huge walled garden at Kilkerran was laid out and tended to perfection. Along one wall was a lean-to greenhouse for raising his tender specimens. It was heated by a coal-fired boiler and was fitted with the best available equipment. Down the opposite wall was a long row of caged pens for the show fowls and the immaculately cultivated beds in the centre produced every sort of vegetable which northern latitudes would allow. The third side gave access to the house and its surrounds and to a cottage known as 'The Wee House' where a gardener lived. The fourth side of the walled garden had a tall, wooden door at its centre which, to the children's disappointment, was always kept locked. It gave access to a little spinney with a steep path of rather perilous stone steps to the foot of the small cliff. Here another locked door gave private access to the stony shore with its intriguing rock pools where eels and crabs could be caught without difficulty.

Below the house was a field, also running down to the shore, known as 'The Battery Park'. Here in Victorian times, the local militia manned the artillery battery which covered the entrance to Campeltown Loch between the mainland and Davaar Island. A small stone building at the foot of the park was the 'Powder House' and was still known as such though it now stored Sandy Ollar's garden lime and other fertilizers rather than gunpowder. Four huge cannons, divested of their carriages, still lay along the boundary with the shore almost concealed by grass and undergrowth. The flowerbeds around the house and down the main drive were a blaze of colour in the spring and summer causing passers-by to stop and peer in awe through gates and hedges.

Alec aged about seven. His cap tally is from the Australian Chatham Class Light Cruiser HMAS *Sydney* **which was stationed at Greenock and in Scapa Flow at various times during World War 1.**

There was a tower in the main house with a room which had a window looking out to sea but was completely sealed with no door. It was said that this once had a navigational light indicating the safe course to enter the harbour but for children, of course, it was the means of numerous gruesome theories about bodies sealed in the room and ghostly faces appearing at the window on stormy nights!

Opposite the house was the old Kilkerran cemetery where generations of Alec's forebears lay – Johnstons, MacAlisters and Ollars – and behind this the great bulk of *Ben Ghullian* rose to the skyline. Halfway up a cluster of rocks marked the entrance to 'The Piper's Cave' where a lovelorn piper was said to have entered with his dog and was never seen again though his dog emerged several days later, without any hair, from a cave at nearby Southend! The haunting lilt of bagpipes could still sometimes be heard at the mouth of the cave by people of sufficient sensitivity!

After their arrival at Kilkerran in 1915, the children's mother stayed on for a few months to see them properly settled in with their new family and at new schools in Campbeltown and then returned to India leaving Liverpool in the SS *City of Poona* on 22nd January 1916.

In this idyllic setting Alec and his sister grew up, fussed over by the maiden aunts and led firmly along the paths of industry and Christian behaviour by a grandfather who was a pillar of the community and a strong disciplinarian. At school, Alec's performance was adequate if not exceptional, but there was one field in which he showed great promise.

From the earliest age he had shown a special aptitude for shooting. His uncle Big Alec, himself an excellent shot, had taken the boy under his wing from the age of six. Shooting at targets in the 'Battery Park', always under strict supervision, taught him the basic rules of handling a rifle. With a bolt-action .22 he developed an extremely high standard of marksmanship and by the age of seven he could, with deadly precision and over open sights, pick off the rats as they emerged from the sewage outfall pipe on the shore.

At eight, Big Alec introduced him to shotguns and taught him the different techniques between rifles and guns. At nine he was allowed out with the guns on an organised shoot for the first time. He gave the boy a beautiful little double-barreled .410 hammer gun which was his pride and

Outside the Summer House at Kilkerran. Alec was brought up with guns and shooting from an early age.

joy. However, for his first season with the guns Big Alec would not allow him any cartridges; he had first to demonstrate that safety procedures were like second nature to him, and his uncle watched him carefully to make sure he broke his gun when going through gates or over stiles and observed all other precautions and conventions. Though it would be several years before he could move on to a large-bore gun, at the age of nine he was known as a useful hand on a rough shoot at which no rabbit would escape his pin sharp observation and hairline response.

Alec and his sister Mary received an excellent basic education at the Campbeltown school but in 1923, when he was 13, his parents decided he would benefit from moving on to a boarding school. His mother arrived from India to make the arrangements and to see him installed for the Michaelmas Term at a boarding school in Edinburgh. When she returned to India in October 1923 she took Mary with her. Mary was 15 and was sent to complete her education at 'Auckland House', a girls' boarding school in Simla, the summer capital of the British Raj in the foothills of the Himalayas.

Little is known of Alec's final years at school and his early years of employment in Edinburgh. What we do know is that his mother and sister returned to Scotland in 1928 for his matriculation. We also know that for his 21st birthday on 3rd December 1931 his father, whom he had not seen since he was five years old, gave him a beautiful matched pair of second-hand, side-by-side hammerless English guns by Holland and Holland, one of the best gunsmiths in the world.

It is unlikely that Alec had many opportunities of double-gun days but his reputation as a useful gun who could be depended upon to swell the bag had certainly spread through the Western Highlands. He was invited as far east as Inverness and as far north as Sutherland and on the occasional double-gun day he now had the finest equipment.

In May 1939 Alec was working for the North British and Mercantile Insurance Company in their Head Office at 64 Prince's Street, Edinburgh. Today, he would no doubt be described as an 'executive', a 'team member' or a 'customer care consultant' but in those days a clerk was called a clerk! With the dark clouds of war thickening over Europe, and Britain's ultimate involvement almost inevitable, Alec and several of his friends decided it was time they were in uniform. The air seemed to him to be the battlefield of the future and so on 30th May 1939 he enlisted in the Royal Air Force Volunteer Reserve (RAFVR) as an Aircraftman Second Class (AC2) with a request that he should be considered for aircrew duties. He was told that at 28 he was too old for pilot training but he could apply to be trained as a navigator, wireless operator or air gunner.

With his background and experience of guns and his proven skills in their use, there could only be one choice.

* * *

An early photograph of the village of Pyrehne where Helmut Lent was born.

In the early hours of 13th June 1918, when Alec was eight and attending school in Campbeltown, the wife of the Pastor of Pyrehne, a village in the far east of Germany, gave birth to her fifth child. He was christened Helmut Johannes Siegfried Lent. His two elder brothers were Werner and Joachim and his elder sisters Käthe and Ursula.

The village of Pyrehne lies in an area of flat, marshy land known at the time as the *Wartebruch*. It was an area of small mixed farms and orchards, in places not unlike parts of England, with narrow, grass verged lanes and spinneys of broadleafed trees.

Like Alec, young Helmut was brought up in a family with strong Christian beliefs and principles. Both families provided an ordered and disciplined way of life with set times for meals at which children were expected to behave with decorum and to eat whatever was put before them. Bad manners of any kind and lack of consideration for others were not tolerated in either family.

When he was nearly six years of age, Helmut was sent to the local primary school, or *Volksschule*, which he attended until he was nearly ten. His father then withdrew him for some cramming at home under his own tutelage, with some assistance from Helmut's elder brothers, for his entry into the *Staatliches Reformgymnasium* at Landsberg – equivalent to a British grammar school.

From an early age, Helmut had shown a passion for military order and precision and in 1933 at the age of fifteen he joined the *Jungvolk* which was the junior branch of the *Hitlerjugend* or Hitler Youth. His powers of leadership were soon recognised and he was appointed *Jungzugführer* in charge of a group of about 20 boys. The following year he was promoted to *Fähnleinführer*, a troop leader with 60 or 70 boys under his command.

In 1935, at the age of seventeen, Helmut passed his *Arbitur*, the equivalent of matriculation in Britain at the time, and commenced his *Reichsarbeitsdienst*, an 8-week period of compulsory community service which had to be completed before a boy could join the armed services. It had always been his intention to apply for officer training in the *Lufwaffe* and his chances were greatly increased by events in that year. The Treaty of Versailles at the end of the First World War prohibited Germany from building up a military air force. For some years they had covertly been doing just this but in 1935, supported by a wave of national pride and patriotism, they discarded all pretence of conformity with the Treaty and began openly to mass produce military aircraft. New aircraft required new aircrews and ground crews and recruitment started in earnest.

On 1st April 1936 Helmut reported to the *Luftkriegsschule*, Air Warfare School, at Gatow in south-west Berlin where he was enrolled as a *Fahnenjunker* or Officer Cadet. Three weeks later he swore the National Socialist Oath of Allegiance. After six months he was promoted to *Fahnenjunker-Gefreiter* and then to *Fahnenjunker-Unteroffizier* after a further two months.

The training course for *Luftwaffe* pilots lasted one year and ten months at the end of which successful trainees would be awarded their flying badge or *Flugzeugführerabzeichen*, equivalent to an RAF pilot's 'Wings'. The qualification was in two parts – the 'A' Licence which covered single-engined aircraft and the 'B' Licence for multi-engined aircraft. Initial flying training was in the Heinkel He72 *Kadett,* which was similar to the Tiger Moth, before moving on to the Focke-Wulf Fw44 *Stieglitz*. Cadets were also taught to drive cars and ride motorcycles during which training Lent broke his leg in an accident which grounded him for five months.

Heinkel He72 Kadett, the Luftwaffe's basic trainer in the 1930s.

After one year's service cadets were promoted to *Fähnrich* and then to *Oberfähnrich* shortly before their commissioning. So on 1st March 1938, having completed his course successfully and received his *Flugzeugführerabzeichen*, Helmut Lent was commissioned as a *Leutnant* in the *Luftwaffe*.

* * *

In a series of outrageous international manoeuvres during the last half of the 1930s, Adolf Hitler had shown that all-out war in Europe would ultimately be inevitable. After his violation of the Treaty of Versailles in rearming the *Luftwaffe* in 1935, he followed up with a further treaty violation in remilitarizing the Rhineland the following year. In November 1936 the newly equipped *Luftwaffe* had its first operational test when the notorious Condor Legion was sent to aid Franco's nationalist forces in the Spanish Civil War. For the pilots involved it was an excellent dress rehearsal for what was to come. At home in Germany, in December, it became compulsory for all boys between the ages of 10 and 18 to join the Hitler Youth.

In March 1938 Germany annexed Austria. Despite continual warnings from Winston Churchill and others, Britain, as usual, had done nothing to prepare herself for war and was in no position to threaten Germany or anyone else. After six months of alternate blustering and feeble supplication Britain, together with France and Italy, signed the Munich Agreement with Germany which effectively gave Hitler *carte blanche* to annex the Sudetenland. This U-shaped strip of lands running round three sides of the border between Germany and the new state of Czechoslovakia contained most of that country's defences and much of her heavy industry. The Agreement, regarded in Czechoslovakia as an act of betrayal, therefore rendered the country incapable of defending itself from further inroads. On 30th September 1938 the British Prime Minister, Neville Chamberlain, believing that this dishonourable pact had appeased Hitler, returned to Britain giving his famous "peace in our time" statement on arrival.

On the same day, as part of a German show of strength over the Sudetenland, Helmut Lent flew his first operational flight in an Arado Ar 72, a single engined biplane. His unit then underwent a conversion course to the Messerschmitt bf108 and bf109 in time to support Germany's annexation of two further provinces of Czechoslovakia, Bohemia and Moravia, in March 1939.

Arado Ar72, an aircraft in which Helmut Lent made his first operational flight as part of a show of strength over the newly-annexed Sudetanland.

At this stage the infant *Luftwaffe* was trying to establish a workable structure for its bomber and fighter forces. It was decided that the fighter force should be divided into *leichte*, light, units equipped with the single engined Messerschmitt bf109 and *schwere*, heavy, units with the larger Messerschmitt bf110. In May 1939 Lent's unit began conversion to the *schwere* role and on 7th June he had his first flight in a bf110, the aircraft with which he would always be most associated.

The bf110C-1 with which the unit was equipped, was powered by two Daimler-Benz DB601A engines and armed with two 20 mm forward-facing cannon, four 7.9 mm MG17 machine guns in the nose and a single rearward-facing MG15 machine gun which could be trained and laid by the second crew member who sat back-to-back with the pilot in the rear of the glazed crew compartment. He was known as the *funker* and was the radio operator as well as the gunner. A *Gefreiter* (equivalent to a Leading Aircraftman in the RAF) Walter Kubisch was assigned as Lent's *funker* and they remained together for most of the war proving, in due course, to be an extremely effective team. The bf110C-1 had an economical cruising speed of 217 mph but was capable of 295 mph at sea level or 336 mph at 20,000 ft. when pressed. Though it could not compete with the faster and more manoeuvrable British fighters such as the Hurricane and Spitfire, in the nightfighter role later in the war the bf110, or *Zerstörer* (Destroyer), as it was called would more than justify its title.

On 25th August 1939 Lent's *staffel*, or squadron, I./2G76, moved to Ohlau, an airfield in lower Silesia close to the Polish border. It was common knowledge among the aircrew that the invasion of Poland was imminent and there was a high state of excitement throughout the *staffel*. On the evening of 31st August Lent and most of his fellow officers were lying on their beds listening to the latest news. The *staffelkapitan*, *Oberleutnant* Werner Hansen, returning from a commanders' briefing, poked his head round the door and whispered: "It's on for tomorrow."

It is unlikely that any of the pilots got much sleep that night and they were awoken at 0230 hrs and told to prepare for an address by *Hauptmann* Gunther Reinecke, the *gruppenkommandeur*. Reinecke told them that take-off was scheduled for 0430 and their task was to escort a force of Heinkel He111 bombers which would attack the airfield at Krakow

Above: **Messerschmitt bf109s in France, August 1940. The bf109 was the principal single-engined fighter of the *leichte* (light) force whereas the twin-engined bf110** *(below)* **was the mainstay of the *schwere* (heavy) force together with the Junkers Ju88** *(inset).*

at 0530. He emphasised that they were about to make history and reminded them of their duty although, being in a state of high enthusiasm and national pride, they needed no reminding.

After their briefing there was still plenty of time left but most of the crews went straight to their aircraft where they sat endlessly checking their aircraft and equipment and waiting for the order to go. At last Lent's section leader gave him the signal to start engines.

"Everything OK?" he asked Walter Kubisch, his *funker*, and on receiving an affirmative reply he opened his throttles and taxied out to the runway behind his leader. Lent took off at 0444 hrs and one minute later German land troops crossed the border into Poland. There had been no formal declaration of war but the invasion had started. Wave after wave of German aircraft bombed the airfield at Krakow; there was a little very inaccurate defensive ground fire and Lent's *staffel* patrolled overhead to deal with any intervention from enemy fighters; but there was none and they returned to base unblooded. The *Luftwaffe* had 1,250 modern aircraft whereas the Polish air force had about 350 obsolescent machines 160 of which were fighters; it was never an even match.

The following day, 2nd September, Britain and France issued a joint ultimatum to Germany to withdraw her forces from Polish territory and the British government introduced immediate conscription for all males between 18 and 41. Hitler ignored the ultimatum and at 11.30 am the next day, 3rd September 1939, Mr Chamberlain announced to the Nation that the ultimatum had expired at 11 o'clock and that Britain was consequently at war with Germany.

Helmut Lent playing cards as he awaits a call to scramble.

Chapter 3 – First Blood

Germany was not long in responding to Britain's Declaration of War: within hours the submarine U.30 had sunk the British passenger liner ss *Athenia* on passage from Glasgow to Toronto with the loss of 112 passengers and crew. Also within hours the governments of Australia, New Zealand, India and Newfoundland, which was yet to become a part of Canada, rallied round the mother country and declared war. South Africa followed suit on the 6th and Canada on the 10th. Italy and the Republic of Ireland declared their neutrality though some 80,000 southern Irish volunteers nevertheless rushed to join the Colours.

On 2nd September 1939 AC2 Alec Ollar reported to Headquarters Reserve Command in Edinburgh to commence his military training. On the same day *Leutnant* Helmut Lent, already on active service, had his first kill when he shot down a Polish PZL24, a high-wing monoplane fighter, over Lódz. He was awarded the Iron Cross 2nd Grade, one of the first ten awarded in the war.

Two days later on 4th September the first British offensive action of the war was undertaken when 15 Blenheims and 14 Wellingtons carried out attacks on German warships. In Wilhelmshaven harbour the cruiser *Emden* suffered some damage when one of the Blenheims crashed on top of it and the pocket battleship *Admiral Scheer* was hit by three bombs all of which failed to explode. Seven of the British aircraft were destroyed by flak and fighters, their crews representing the first of the 55,000 airmen killed in Bomber Command during the war. Targets for bombing were necessarily limited at this stage as British aircraft were not permitted to fly over neutral Belgium and Holland, and France, in fear of retaliation, would not allow Britain to mount attacks on German cities from French soil. The bombers therefore had to take the much longer route to the north German coast. Nor were they permitted to bomb anywhere where civilian casualties might be caused so their targets were limited to German warships, but only those under way or moored in open waters. If they were tied up in dock an attack could result in civilian casualties so was therefore prohibited. While

POLSKA LOTNICZA, WARSAW 1937

**A Polish PZL24 fighter aircraft of the type shot down by Helmut Lent
on 2nd September 1939 – his first victory!**

these restrictions prevailed, the only other action which Bomber Command could take was the distribution of propaganda leaflets over Germany which it undertook on a regular basis.

On 17th September the Soviet Union invaded Poland from the east and by the middle of October, after heroic resistance, the remnants of this gallant and ill-used nation surrendered. Helmut Lent's *staffel*, no longer required in Poland, moved back to Stuttgart for defence of the Reich.

During the first eight months of conflict, to be known later as 'the phoney war', there was a stand-off position in Europe between the land forces of Britain and Germany with each side seemingly unwilling to commit itself to a full-scale offensive. However, this was not the case at sea. Well before the declaration of war, Germany had sent U-boats out into the Atlantic so they would be ready to attack Britain's trade routes as soon as war broke out. By the end of the year they had already achieved significant success; as well as merchant shipping, U-boats had sunk HMS *Courageous*, an aircraft carrier, and HMS *Royal Oak*, a battleship, as she lay at anchor in Scapa Flow. In addition to the U-boats, the *Kriegsmarine*, German navy, also had some formidable surface raiders in a new class of pocket battleship which threatened to wreak havoc in the Atlantic shipping routes. With Britain dependent on overseas trade for her survival, it was these surface raiders which became the first priority for Bomber Command's operations.

On 19th December, in the course of one such operation, an air battle was fought which would prove to be a key turning point in aerial warfare and was to change the entire strategy of Bomber Command. Up until that time every operation had been planned on the assumption that "the bomber will always get through." Bombers flew in tight, self-defending formations so the group had a line of fire in all directions and the aircraft on the outside of the group would protect those on the inside. This, to some extent, was effective but the practice made no allowance for what would happen if the formation broke up or was dispersed, or depleted, by enemy ground fire. It was a lesson which was to be learnt the hard way.

Aircraft from three squadrons, Nos. 9, 37 and 214, comprising a force of 24 Wellingtons, took off on the morning of 19th December with orders to attack enemy warships off the north German port of Wilhelmshaven within the restrictions regarding civilian casualties already mentioned. Two aircraft had to turn back due to engine trouble so 22 reached the target after a circuitous route which brought them in from the

**A Junkers Ju52/3m flies over Helmut Lent's Messerschmitt bf110
which has overrun the runway at Oslo-Fornebu in April 1940
and come to rest in the garden of a private house.**

east rather than the west. This, they hoped, would give them the element of surprise but, unfortunately for them, a team demonstrating the German *Freya* radar detected their approach, purely by chance, when they were some 30 miles offshore. The *Luftwaffe,* though they could scarcely believe that the RAF would be mounting a daylight raid in perfect, clear weather conditions, eventually scrambled around 40 fighters, twice the number of bombers, with instructions to attack the formations from the beam rather than from the rear where they could be coned with fire from the rear gunners of the formation. It was thought that several bombs dropped by the Wellingtons had hit enemy warships off the coast but they were unable to observe and confirm the results.

As the bombers climbed away from the target, following the period of intense concentration in ensuring that their bombs were dropped accurately and distracted, no doubt, by ground fire, the tight formation started to break up and attempts to restore it only made matters worse. As soon as the ground fire had ceased, the German fighters dived in and inflicted heavy losses shooting down 11 out of 22 of the bombers, the bf109s accounting for 7 and the bf110s for 4. Three enemy aircraft were destroyed and several damaged by defensive fire from the Wellingtons. *Oberleutnant* Johann Fuhrmann flying a bf109 failed in his beam attack on the formation so, against his instructions, tried attacking from the rear. He was shot down and was drowned trying to swim to shore from his ditched aircraft.

On the morning of the 19th Helmut Lent was on a routine patrol from his base at Jever, when he received a radio message that a force of British bombers were attacking German warships off Wilhelmshaven. He altered course for Heligoland and when he reached the battle the British aircraft had dropped their bombs and were just off Borkum in the East Frisian Islands heading home on a north-westerly course. They had broken formation and were flying singly or in small, ragged groups making themselves easy prey for the fighters. Several had already been shot down and Lent lost no time in making his first attack on a Wellington of 37 Squadron which he disabled when its starboard engine burst into flames. The aircraft managed to glide down and ditch in the shallow waters off Borkum and the pilot, Flying Officer P A Wimberley, was captured and became a prisoner of war. This was the first British aircraft that Lent had shot down.

Eight minutes later, with his fuel running low, he closed in on another of the bombers. His first attack failed to disable it so he turned round and came in for a second attempt. As he closed in on his prey he came under heavy fire from the rear gunner but the comparatively puny .303 machine guns of the Wellington were no match for the 20 mm cannon of the *Zerstorer* and the bomber burst into flames and fell away into the sea. However, the rear gunner of the doomed bomber had riddled the German aircraft with fire during the engagement and its starboard engine suddenly cut out. Lent was also alarmed to see that the ammunition for his forward machine guns was on fire and thick black smoke was pouring into the cabin. Then his port engine stopped. His first reaction was to order his *funker* to bale out and then follow him but when he looked at the sea below, which was a mass of ice floes, he realised that their chances of survival would be slight. He therefore decided to attempt a long glide towards the nearest land which he estimated might be just within his range. Thanks to a favourable wind and the fact that he had plenty of height at the start of his glide, he was able to make a miraculous landing at the little airfield on the Island of Wangerooge.

As a loyal German officer, Helmut was naturally proud of his achievements but he also felt a sincere compassion for his fallen foes. In a letter to his parents on the same day he told them how he wished he could have dropped his rubber dinghy for the English crew but that they had either been burned to death or drowned. "War is nonsensical:" he wrote, "first you shoot them down and then you want to help them."

His second victim of the day was a Wellington 1A of 37 Squadron flown by 24 year-old Flying Officer Oliver Lewis, an Australian from Sydney. He and his crew were all killed when their aircraft crashed close inshore on the Island of Borkum. A few weeks later, a *Kriegsmarine* NCO who was in the party which recovered the bodies sent Helmut a photograph of the wreckage which he had taken half an hour after the crash. In another letter home Helmut told his family that he was particularly pleased to learn that the British airmen had been buried with full military honours and that a ribbon on the wreath read: "To a brave enemy."

Of the eleven Wellingtons which limped home, three had to make crash landings on English soil so only eight out of the original 24, one third, made it back to their home stations. As a consequence of the enquiries and debates which followed the battle, the concept of the tight-formation, self-defending bomber force was abandoned and daylight raids were never again attempted except for attacks on specific targets on rare occasions. A basic design flaw in the Wellington was also identified and corrected; the tendency of these aircraft to catch fire very early in an engagement was attributed to their lack of self-sealing fuel tanks and the entire Wellington force was consequently modified.

From the German side, lessons were also learnt from the Battle of the German Bight as it was known in Germany. It confirmed the fact that the Wellington was no match for the bf110 when attacks were made from the flank or from directly ahead. They had learned that the Wellington caught fire very easily and that the sting in the tail should be avoided.

* * *

A captured Messerschmitt bf110C-4 which was forced to land by gunfire at Goodwood in 1940.

RAF OFFICIAL PHOTOGRAPH

In September 1939 Alexander Ollar having attended a two-day aircrew assessment in Edinburgh and, having passed the aircrew selection board, was inducted into the RAFVR. After a series of medicals and inoculations he was sworn in and then posted to Grangemouth to start his initial training with the basic Air Observer Course. His wage as an AC2 was 4 shillings a day (20 new pence in today's currency) which would increase to 6 shillings and 6 pence when he was fully trained.

At Grangemouth he was issued with his uniforms, mess tin, cutlery and enamel mug. He was also given a cardboard carton in which to send his civilian clothes home. He was an airman now! Alec made his first ever flight on 12th October in an Avro Anson flying over Loch Earn and Perth and during the next two weeks, as part of the Course, he flew over many parts of Scotland which he knew intimately from the ground – Callander, Loch Tay, Oban and Stirling and all the hills and glens between. On these

**Edinburgh RAFVR Intake Grangemouth September 1939.
Alec is third from left in centre row.**

**Recruit Taining School Padgate February 1940.
Alec is second from left in back row.**

training flights trainees were introduced to map reading and elementary navigation.

From Grangemouth Alec was posted to the Recruit Training School at Padgate. Initial training consisted of daily drill parades, physical training and cross-country runs all under the scrutiny and direction of stentorian long-service NCOs whose job it was to turn sloppy, soft civilians into hard and disciplined servicemen. Trainees also received lectures on general aviation and the history and traditions of the RAF. They were also taught to fire the .303 Lee Enfield service rifle at which Alec, naturally enough, achieved top marks and to take their turn at guard duty around the camp perimeter at night with a rifle slung on their shoulder though they were not yet trusted with ammunition!

Having completed his basic training in March 1940, Alec was posted to No. 8 Bombing and Gunnery School at Evanton in Easter Ross to start specialist gunnery training and he was soon to learn that there was far more to an air gunner's job than being able to aim and fire a machine gun.

'A' Squad No. 8 Bombing and Gunnery School, Evanton, May 1940.
Alec back row left and Sergeant Parrott middle row centre.

First of all they had to know their guns inside out and back to front and to this end were required to strip down and reassemble a Browning .303 on almost every day of their six-week course until they knew every part by feel and the procedure had become second nature to them. They were considered competent when they could strip down and reassemble a gun in two minutes when blindfolded, to simulate a situation where electric power had been lost during combat. They were also taught the importance of cleaning and maintaining their weapons and were required to be familiar with the ammunition for their guns and with all pyrotechnic devices, such as flares, currently in use in the Service.

The theory of air gunnery was explained in classroom lectures and trainees were taught how to recognise all the aircraft, hostile and friendly, which they were likely to encounter during operations. Images and silhouettes at different angles and distances were projected on to a screen until the trainees could identify them instantly. Once identified and confirmed as a target, they were taught how to estimate the distance of the aircraft. For Alec, another dimension had been added; he was experienced at judging distances and shooting at moving targets in a two-dimensional world, now he had to add height into the equation.

First trainees had to learn how to 'harmonise' their guns – that is to adjust the toe-in so the two streams of bullets converge at the optimum distance. Later, when experienced, individual gunners might wish to harmonise their guns to suit their own style of shooting but at this stage they were adjusted to the standard RAF settings. In aiming their guns they had to consider that they were firing from a moving platform to a moving target both of which were travelling at different speeds and on different courses and were usually at different heights. To be sure of hitting the target, gunners were taught how to estimate the 'angle off' which was the angle between the enemy aircraft's course and the gunner's line of sight; unless this angle was zero it was necessary to aim off at a point where the gunner predicted the target would be by the time the bullets reached it. They also had to estimate 'bullet drop' – the longer the range the more vertical elevation the gunner needed to allow for the slight downward curve of his fire. To enable him to see where his fire was going, tracers were inserted in the ammunition belts, normally one tracer for every five rounds. The temptation to 'hosepipe', or to keep firing as if the stream of bullets was water from a hosepipe, had to be resisted; a one-second burst of fire used ten rounds and ammunition was not unlimited. It was therefore essential that trainee gunners thoroughly mastered the theory and techniques of aerial gunnery before they began putting the theory into practice with live firing.

As well as the guns themselves, the air gunner had to become thoroughly familiar with the operation of the gun turrets. There were three makes of turret in use with the RAF – Boulton-Paul, Fraser-Nash and Bristol – and a basic knowledge of all three was necessary as the trainee could find himself in any one of them when he eventually reached his squadron. Then there were four turret positions – tail, nose, mid-upper and mid-lower; each required a different position and different aiming techniques although their basic operation was much the same. On operations a gunner would normally settle into the position in which he proved himself best but still had to be prepared to man any of the other positions if necessary. Turrets were rotated by electrical or hydraulic power from the aircraft's engines which could be cut off due to combat damage so emergency systems and procedures also had to be learnt.

For training purposes turrets were mounted on large 4-wheeled trailers with power to the turrets provided by petrol engines mounted behind. These trailers were positioned in a line while a 'target' aircraft would dive and fly low over the airfield while trainees 'shot' at them. Cine cameras monitored the accuracy of fire for later examination by the instructors.

The instructor for Alec's squad of ten students was a Sergeant Parrott a calm, time-served, regular airman, seldom seen without his pipe in his mouth, who was a well respected and very competent teacher. He would take infinite care to ensure that even the weaker members of his squad understood each stage of tuition before moving on to the next. There were two students, Alec and another Scot, Archie Roberts, who had been manager of an insurance office in Glasgow, who had had extensive shooting experience in civilian life and tended to pick things up faster than the rest; their performance was also better and their fellows tended to turn to them for assistance if they were having difficulties with any part of the curriculum. Sergeant Parrott was proud of his two star pupils and made sure

Sergeant Parrott and his two "star pupils!" –
Archie Roberts *(left)* **and Alec** *(right).*

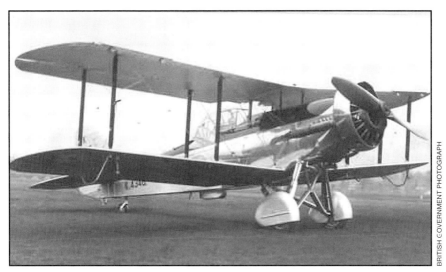

BRITISH GOVERNMENT PHOTOGRAPH

Westland Wallace, one of the aircraft used extensively for gunnery training in 1940 and the first aircraft to fly over Mount Everest.

they were in the practice turrets when an inspecting officer was in the vicinity!

Concurrent with their classroom and ground training at Evanton, students were taken up in mainly Harrow but sometimes Wallace aircraft with the vast open expanse of the Northern Highlands as their training grounds. The Handley Page Harrow was a twin-engined, high-wing, heavy bomber with a fixed undercarriage. Its normal crew was five but for training purposes it could comfortably take the entire squad of ten who would then take it in turns, in each turret position, for live air-to-air and air-to-ground firing, their performance again monitored by cameras attached to the guns. In a typical session each trainee got the opportunity to fire about 300 rounds at a drogue target towed behind another aircraft. The Westland Wallace was a very different proposition. This was a big two-seater biplane which had the distinction of having been the first aeroplane to fly over Mount Everest. It had been in service for the past seven years and was approaching obsolescence in operational roles other than training and target towing. The gunner sat in the open rear cockpit with a single, swiveling .303 machine gun which gave students a real taste of what aerial gunnery had been like in the previous war.

GENERAL HINTS FOR AIR GUNNERS

SEARCH THE SKY BEFORE TAKE OFF AND LANDING
WHEN YOUR AIRCRAFT IS MOST VULNERABLE.

IF GUN FIRE IS OBSERVED SEARCH FOR FIGHTERS
AND TAKE EVASIVE ACTION.

PATROL ACROSS THE SUN, NEVER INTO IT OR AWAY FROM IT.

IF USING TRACER AT NIGHT, REMEMBER IT TENDS TO
MOMENTARILY DESTROY YOUR NIGHT VISION;
HOLD YOUR FIRE IF NECESSARY.

THE AIM OF AN ENEMY FIGHTER IS TO DESTROY;
THE AIM OF A BOMBER AIR GUNNER IS TO GET SAFELY TO THE TARGET
AND BACK TO BASE.

NEVER FIRE UNTIL FIRED UPON, IN THE EVENT OF GUNFIRE
SEARCH FOR FIGHTER AND TAKE EVASIVE ACTION.

ALWAYS WATCH YOUR OWN TAIL.

CONSERVE YOUR AMMO; IF YOU ARE FIRED UPON FROM
LONG-RANGE INSTRUCT THE PILOT TO TAKE EVASIVE ACTION.

NEVER FLY STRAIGHT OR DIVE WHEN UNDER ATTACK;
NEVER TURN AWAY FROM AN ATTACK, ALWAYS TOWARD.

USE GOOD TEAM WORK WITH THE REST OF THE CREW.

IF ON RECONNAISSANCE AIRCRAFT, YOUR JOB IS TO RETURN WITH
INFORMATION; NOT TO SEEK COMBAT WITH ENEMY AIRCRAFT.

ALL AIRCRAFT APPROACHING ARE CONSIDERED TO BE ENEMY
UNTIL IDENTIFIED OTHERWISE.

IF YOUR OWN GUNS FAIL OR ARE DAMAGED DURING AN ATTACK
USE YOUR INGENUITY TO OUTWIT THE ATTACKER.

REMEMBER:
TO BE SURPRISED IS TO BE LOST

Guidance from the Gunnery Course Manual.

Alec passed out from Evanton, with an above average rating, on 5th May 1940 and was posted to No. 15 OTU, Operational Training Unit, at Harwell near Oxford for specialist training on the Wellington bomber in which he would be flying on completion of this course. On 20th May he was promoted to sergeant. From Harwell he was able to spend occasional weekends with his sister, Mary, who had married a regular officer in the Royal Tank Regiment in Calcutta and now lived with their two children in a house near the barracks in Farnborough, Hampshire. Alec bought a second-hand motorcycle from another airman who had been posted away which enabled him to do the journey much quicker, and more reliably, than by train.

The OTU at Harwell provided a concentrated three-week course in which trainees went up for at least one flight, sometimes two and occasionally three, on almost every weekday. The flights normally lasted for between two and four hours during which the gunner had the opportunity of some serious shooting, usually firing 600 or 700 rounds and on one long flight of six hours 1,000 rounds. Alec had his first flight in a Wellington on 18th June as he was to join a squadron equipped with Wellingtons. He had also developed a proclivity for the rear gun turret which decided his position for the remainder of his training and eventually on operational flights.

By the end of this short but intensive course Alec felt completely at home in the rear turret of a Wimpy and could lay his hands on everything he needed even in pitch darkness simulating a power failure. On 20th June he even had a real-life emergency drill when engine trouble forced the pilot, Flying Officer Davidson, to make a forced landing at Sealand west of Chester.

On 8th July Alec had his last training flight of five hours in a Wellington N3016 flown by Sergeant Pilot Wessels. The following day Sergeant Ollar passed out as a fully-trained air gunner and received his coveted AG single-wing brevet.

Aircraftsman Ollar with his newly acquired Air Gunner's brevet.

By the end of 1939 the German propaganda machine, always on the lookout for heroes whom they could publicise to inspire the youth of the country, had singled out Helmut Lent. As a good-looking, Aryan, *Luftwaffe* ace he fitted their requirements perfectly and they had turned him into a minor hero. As a result, he regularly received unsolicited letters from uninhibited young women containing proposals ranging from requests for a signed photograph to immediate marriage. Some of the girls were clearly deranged and most of the letters he ignored but one day he received one which caught his attention and which he decided to follow up. It was from an Elisabeth Peterson who lived in Hamburg, not far from his base at Jever, and he arranged to meet her for a 'blind date' at the Reichshof Hotel in Hamburg where they had dinner together and were clearly attracted to each other.

Elisabeth, however, was not all that she seemed: her real name was Lena Senokosnikova and she had been born in Moscow from where her father, a wealthy merchant, had fled during the Russian Revolution of 1918 to be followed three years later by Lena, her mother and her sister. Lena was naturally dark but had dyed her hair blonde to try and look as Aryan as possible for her meeting with Helmut. She worked for her father's firm in Hamburg.

Notwithstanding her deceptions, of which Helmut soon became aware, a romantic relationship developed between them and in February 1940 they went on a skiing holiday together to Hirschegg, an Alpine village in Austria. Both Helmut and Lena were extremely apprehensive as to how she would be accepted by his family; she was four years older than Helmut and Russians were generally despised in the Third Reich. Though they may well have had their misgivings, their brave son's happiness was paramount to Helmut's parents and when they realised how strong his feelings were for her, they welcomed her into the family.

Alec, too, had for some time had a romantic involvement. Since the previous year he had been walking out with a secretary who worked for North British & Mercantile in the same office as himself in Prince's Street, Edinburgh. Agnes Gilzean, always known as Nessie, was the daughter of Councillor Andrew Gilzean a prominent citizen who was eventually to become Labour Member of Parliament for Edinburgh Central. As with Helmut and Lena, Nessie was a few years older than Alec and the political uncertainty during 1939 had deterred them from any plans of marriage for the time being.

However, in July 1940 when Alec had qualified as an air gunner and had been promoted to Sergeant, they decided not to wait any longer and were married in Edinburgh on 22nd July. To Alec's great disappointment, his best friend, Murray Collins, who had been a colleague at North British before the war, was unable to attend; he had been commissioned in the Royal Artillery and could not obtain leave. Alec himself had only got nine days leave, to include his travelling time, so their wartime honeymoon was a necessarily rushed affair with most of it spent at Kilkerran, principally to introduce Nessie to his family.

THE SCOTSMAN

EDINBURGH, WEDNESDAY, JULY 24, 1940.

Marriage

OLLAR—GILZEAN.—At Palmerston Place Church, EDINBURGH, on 22nd July 1940, by the Rev. Wm. C. Macdonald, M.A., Sergeant ALEXANDER J. S. OLLAR, R.A.F., only son of Mr and Mrs Stewart Ollar, Calcutta, to AGNES McNEIL, second daughter of Councillor and Mrs ANDREW GILZEAN, 4 Bernard Terrace, Edinburgh.

By now both his grandparents were dead and the eldest of the aunts, Minnie, had died the year before. Aunt Kate had left Campbeltown to follow a career in the south and Uncle Ronald, who had been very seriously wounded in Flanders in World War 1 and had never regained his health, had died at Kilkerran a few years previously. This left Aunt Martha, now the senior lady of the family, and Big Alec the only surviving uncle who had been too old to enlist but, anxious to do something for the war effort, had enrolled as a Special Constable for the duration.

Martha and Big Alec, like generations of their family before them, were ardent supporters of the Conservative and Unionist Party and Martha was deeply involved in the business of the local committee. The news that Wee Alec had married the daughter of a Labour politician was therefore not well received and a distinctly frigid atmosphere existed for the few days they spent at Kilkerran which sadly never thawed out though, as with Helmut's parents, a dignified courtesy was maintained.

Chapter 4 – "The Boys who bombed Berlin"

A lec was posted to 115 Squadron at Marham in Norfolk and made his first operational flight on the night of 14th July 1940. The objective was Vught Airfield in Holland, which was being used as one of the *Luftwaffe's* forward bases, and their bombs were seen to start several fires on the ground. On the way home an enemy aircraft was sighted but it either did not see them or had more important things on its mind.

Marham Aerodrome had first been used in 1916 by the infant Royal Flying Corps and had closed again in 1919 after the war. In 1937 it had been reconstructed as a heavy bomber station and 115 Squadron had moved in during June equipped with Harrow bombers. In 1939 the Squadron had received Wellington Mk1s which they were operating when Alec arrived.

An aerial view of RAF Marham, 1944.

RAF OFFICIAL PHOTOGRAPH

He was crewed up under a Sergeant Pilot Gregory and was delighted to see that the second pilot's place was allocated to a friend of his since Harwell, Sergeant Cyril Wessels, who had actually been his pilot on his last training flight at No. 15 OTU. The navigator was Sergeant Woor and the wireless operator and front gunner were Sergeants Cleverly and Palmer. This was Alec's first experience of the close bond which invariably developed between members of a crew which went into battle together, each being dependent on the others for his safe return. Cyril Wessels was from Hull and, like all British servicemen of German descent, was determined, through his performance, to show his complete loyalty and commitment to Britain.

Through the rest of July and most of August they undertook bombing missions against targets in Germany. On days when Sergeant Gregory was stood down, Sergeant Wessels would take his place. On 27th July they bombed an oil storage depot at Hamburg, on the 30th the marshalling yards at Soest. On 2nd August they were back to the same target in Hamburg with 11 aircraft from each of the two squadrons at Marham. At 0145 am on the 3rd, when Alec's plane was over the North Sea on its way home, an SOS was received at Marham from a Wellington of their sister squadron, No. 38, flown by Pilot Officer Reginald Gerry a 23 year-old Canadian from Calgary. The reception had kept wavering as the aircraft had lost then regained height as its engine cut in an out. The signals continued for half an hour and then silence. Their last reported position was about 100 miles off the coast north-east of Marham. At 0530 Wing Commander Dabinett took off to search for them and the following day Coastal Command joined in the search but nothing was found. The pilot's body was later washed ashore in Holland and was buried at the Oldebruek General Cemetery.

On the 5th a report was received that the German battleship *Gneisnau* was in dock at the Germania Shipyard at Kiel and a force of 27 Wellingtons from Marham, Mildenhall and Stradishall set out to hunt it down. Cloud cover was heavy and it was impossible to locate the target. Three days later they returned to Hamburg acting on a report that the *Bismarck* was there but with 10/10 cloud cover the mission was again unsuccessful.

Crash landing at Hillsden due to shortage of fuel on return from Bordeaux, 14th August 1940. *From left:* **Sergeants Ollar** *(Rear Gunner),* **Woor** *(Navigator),* **Peters** *(Wireless Operator),* **Gregory** *(Pilot),* **Wessels** *(Second Pilot),* and **Palmer** *(Front Gunner).*

On 10th August they attacked the docks at Wilhelmshaven and on 12th the Messerschmitt works at Gotha. After a long 9-hour flight bombing oil depots at Nantes and Bordeaux on the 14th, they had to make a forced landing at Hillsden due to shortage of fuel. Their undercarriage collapsed but nobody was hurt. The target had originally been Cologne but was changed shortly before take-off to Bordeaux. Four of the aircraft had to make forced landings in England and only two managed to scrape home with fuel tanks almost empty. The crews were collected the following afternoon and flown back to Marham as passengers.

During the time that Alec had been completing his training, much had happened in Europe. In April Germany had invaded Norway and set up a puppet government under Vidkun Quisling whose name was to enter the dictionary as a term for a traitor and collaborator. The Norwegians put up a gallant resistance, aided by Britain, but by the end of June were overwhelmed by the might of the *Wehrmacht*.

On 10th May Neville Chamberlain resigned and Winston Churchill became Prime Minister and was called upon to form a wartime coalition government. On the same day Germany invaded Belgium and France with a new technique which they called *Blitzkrieg* – fast moving infantry spearheaded by a concentration of armour. By the end of the month the pathetically outnumbered British Expeditionary Force, which had been sent to Europe to stem the German advance, had been driven back to the sea. *Operation Dynamo*, the miraculous evacuation of some 340,000 British, French and Belgian troops from the beaches at Dunkirk, under continual attack from the *Luftwaffe*, was completed by 3rd June.

Things looked very bad for Britain and one week later Italy, having seen which way the war was progressing, allied itself to what it believed would be the winning side and declared war on Britain and France. France collapsed and surrendered on 25th June and by the end of July Norway, Belgium, Holland, France and Czechoslovakia had all established governments-in-exile in Britain.

Then on 10th July, four days before Alec made his first operational flight, the *Luftwaffe* launched an all-out assault initially on Channel shipping and then on RAF stations in England for the purpose of gaining air superiority in time for *Operation Sealion*, Hitler's invasion of Britain, which he had planned for 15th September. This assault by the *Luftwaffe* was later to be known as the 'Battle of Britain' and as RAF Fighter Command bravely fought off wave after wave of enemy bombers, the date for Hitler's invasion was put back again and again until early September when the *Luftwaffe* abandoned its attacks on airfields in the south-east and turned its attention on London.

During the Battle of Norway Helmut Lent found himself escorting troop-carrying transport aircraft and during April shot down one Norwegian and two British Gloster Gladiators – hopelessly outdated biplanes which were no match for the *Zerstorers* of Lent's *staffel*. While patrolling on 9th April with his *Staffelkapitan*, Werner Hansen, Helmut came upon a Sunderland flying boat from 210 Squadron Invergordon on a reconnaissance flight over the Oslo Fjord. The huge and ponderous flying boat stood no chance against the nimble Messerschmitts and crashed in flames into the fjord killing the

CANADIAN FORCES OFFICIAL PHOTOGRAPH

Short Sunderland Flying Boat.

whole crew except for the wireless operator who, it seems, was thrown clear in the explosion and fell 1,500 feet without a parachute and survived! The pilot of the Sunderland was Flight Lieutenant Peter Kite from Winchmore Hill, Middlesex. He was 20 years old.

Because of the long lines of communication between Germany and Norway, Lent's *staffel* was equipped with a special long-range edition of the *Zerstorer* – the bf110 D-1/R. Due to the bulging extra fuel tanks below the fuselage it was popularly known as the *Dachelbauch* or Dachshund Belly. Helmut was to claim only one further victory during 1940; this was on 15th June when he shot down his first Blenheim over Trondheim; Pilot Officer Peter Gaylard and his crew were all killed.

Bristol Blenheim Mk IV Light Bomber. This particular aircraft was lost with itrs entire crew during a raid on Ostend in September 1940.

RAF OFFICIAL PHOTOGRAPH / B J DAVENTRY

Lent paid his first visit to Britain on 15th August, the day after Alec's Wellington made a forced landing at Hillsden due to shortage of fuel. Helmut's *staffel* was tasked with escorting a formation of Heinkel 111 bombers on a raid over the North-East of England. He was lucky to return as, not only did his aircraft develop engine trouble, but he was set upon by six Spitfires from which he had considerable difficulty in escaping. The only damage he managed to do was to destroy two barrage balloons over Hull.

Following the Battle of the German Bight, when it became clear to the German high command that Britain would no longer undertake daylight raids, Göring had decreed that a *Nachtjagd* or nightfighter force should be formed and trained in the special techniques required to prey successfully on the British bomber streams. To his initial dismay, Lent's *staffel* was selected to be part of the first nightfighter formation and was moved to an airfield in the south of Germany, near Munich, for training. Pilots were instructed in interception tactics and blind flying and at the same time top priority was given to development of an air-to-air radar which would assist them in their task. It was also clear to the German high command that to be most effective the *Nachtjagd* units should be located in Holland on the principal approach and exit routes of the bombers so, on 1st October 1940, Lent and his *staffel* arrived at Deelen airfield to start operations as night-fighters.

On 21st August Sergeant Gregory was posted to Bassingbourn for resting and Alec's crew got a new captain, Sergeant Norman Sydney Lionel Stent. Bomber crews were very conservative and did not like changes in their members.

Sergeant Norman Stent – "A pretty determined bloke."

Marham, September 1940 *From left:* **Sergeants Ollar, Palmer, Woor and Stent.** *Sitting:* **Sergeant Wessels**

The safety of a crew depended to a large extent on the interaction between its members who developed a great trust in and respect for each other's abilities and a newcomer was regarded with some reserve until he had demonstrated his worth. Norman Stent soon proved himself to be a very able and conscientious pilot with whom the other members became completely comfortable after a few operations. Alec wrote to his wife:

> **"Our new captain is a pretty determined bloke, no indiscriminate bombing with him, if they sent him out to bomb a matchbox I quite believe he would hit it but he's a pretty careful flyer just the same."**

And so the all-sergeant crew of Stent, Wessels, Woor, Peters, Palmer and Ollar, each now well experienced and having complete confidence in the proficiency of his fellows, was ready to undertake its most important mission yet.

All this time while Bomber Command had been taking the battle into the enemy heartland, Fighter Command had continued in the defensive role in protecting Britain form the massed onslaughts of the *Luftwaffe* which, so far, had concentrated on Channel shipping and airfields in the East of England. However, on the night of 24th August, German aircraft bombed the Church of St. Giles in Cripplegate, an area right in the centre of London on the old City Wall which today is the site of the brutalist Barbican Estate. It is probable that this was unintentional and was simply an aircraft jettisoning its bombs indiscriminately on its way home. Nevertheless, Churchill was outraged and decreed that vengeance was to be extracted. The following day the order came through to Bomber Command to undertake the previously unthinkable: an attack was to be launched immediately on Berlin.

So the target was Berlin; they were to undertake a raid on the German capital – something that Göring had told Berliners could never possibly happen. This was 28th August 1940. An attempt had been made three days earlier but thick cloud had turned the operation into a fiasco: with around 50 aircraft involved, only one bomb had dropped on Berlin, destroying a wooden summerhouse in the suburbs and inflicting minor injuries on two people! Bomber Command was a laughing stock among Berliners; but they would not laugh for long.

Nine Wellingtons of 115 Squadron were due to take off from 2100. As part of a force of 79 bombers, 115's objectives were Tempelhof Airfield and the electrical works at Klingenberg. A high degree of excitement tempered with apprehension prevailed among the aircrews as they were driven out in lorries to their dispersals. Wellington 'P-Peter', 9285, was handed over to Sergeant Stent's crew by the ground crew who had been working on her for most of the day. Ground crews became very proprietorial with 'their' aircraft and took great pride in maintaining it to the highest standards. They 'lent' it, somewhat reluctantly, to the aircrew who would fly it and expected them to take proper care of it when it was in their charge; if they strained or damaged any of its equipment without good reason, they would receive a very frigid reception from the ground crew.

Alec followed Lionel Stent and Cyril Wessels up the ladder, through the crew hatch and then began making his way back through the

The Rear Gunner of a Wellington Bomber in his turret.

cramped fuselage to the rear gun turret. Every action performed in the Air Force, and indeed in all the armed services, was covered by a drill; even the most simple endeavour like opening a door had been examined and recorded. Although this might have appeared ridiculous to a civilian, the serviceman could be absolutely sure that the way he had been instructed to do anything had been the subject of considerable experience and research and was the result of the perfect compromise between speed, efficiency and safety; moreover, the authorities knew that a drill which had become embedded in the mind would be automatically recalled in an emergency without having to think and waste precious time; foolish was the man who thought he could improve upon 'the book'. Alec, having been brought up with the discipline of guns and shooting, recognised the efficacy of established procedures and always did things in the RAF prescribed way.

When he reached the tail of the aircraft he unlocked and opened the double doors into the gun turret and pulled the safety harness over the ammunition tanks on both sides so he would not sit on them when he got in. Then, holding on to the handrail above him he swung himself feet first through the opening and into the gunner's seat.

Once in he plugged in his intercom jack and made sure it was firmly home then closed the turret doors behind him, left side first then right, locked them and leaned back against them to check they were firmly locked. This was important as the turret could traverse through 90 degrees in the air in which position the doors would open into space rather than the fuselage. Later in the war, the rear gunner would have his parachute in the turret with him and his escape route would be to rotate the turret 90 degrees, open the doors and drop out backwards; in 1940 though, the rear gunner's parachute was stowed in the fuselage and his chances of getting out were slim. Alec then fastened his safety harness pulling the two fabric tongues through their metal stirrups to lock the buckles.

Next he tested and set his reflector sight and checked his ammunition by removing the lids from the tanks and examined the base of the rounds to make sure that the ammunition in both tanks was joined and was being fed from the rear tanks. Beside his left leg was a pocket containing two lengths of flexible wire, one with a wooden toggle at one end and a metal ring at the other and the second with a loop at one end and a flat metal hook at the other. These were the loading toggle and the arming cable and, having checked that they were both in order, he returned them to their stowage. He then checked the position of his seat with the two adjusting handles which were then folded back to their stowed position. His guns and turret were now ready bar for the live test which would be carried out once the aircraft was clear of the land.

'P-Peter' took off at 1937 six minutes behind 'K-King' and 21 minutes ahead of 'D-Dog'. This was to be the longest operational flight they had undertaken and the aircraft was very heavily laden with full fuel tanks and a large bomb load. Quite a collection of ground staff and WAAFs had gathered beside the runway to wave the bombers off – a ritual they would perform faithfully for every operation regardless of the weather. As they roared down the runway Cyril Wessels held both throttles fully open while Norman Stent struggled to keep her straight and lift her clear of the ground against her inclination to crash through the perimeter fence into the fields beyond.

Once airborne, 'P-Peter' started her long climb to operational height and turned on to the course for the Dutch coast worked out by Thomas Woor. Once over the sea, Alec loaded his guns by pulling the rounds up into the feed opening with the arming cable he had earlier checked; he then detached the cable and pressed down on the last link before closing the breech cover and returning the arming cable to its proper stowage. He then withdrew the other cable from its pocket, hooked the ring over the cocking stud on the guns then pulled back on the toggle until a loud click confirmed that the gun was cocked. He then repeated this operation before calling through to the captain on the intercom for permission to test fire his guns.

Having received an affirmative answer, Alec moved the 'Fire/Safe' switch to 'Fire' and fired a test burst into the sea below. Having ensured that hand rotation was disengaged he then reported his guns OK and ready to the Captain.

Alec now takes up the story in a letter to Nessie two days later:

"We had the usual quiet run to the Dutch coast. As soon as we got to the Zuider Zee the fun started and we were more or less under fire and bothered with searchlights for the 200-odd mile trip to Berlin. There was no mistaking Berlin – I've never seen such a concentration of searchlights and A.A. fire. The weather was perfect except for a slight ground haze. Our target was the marshalling yards at Goerlitzer (that's the station Mussolini arrived at

SGT DOUG PALMER
SGT ALLAN RICHARDSON
SGT HOLLINGWORTH
SGT ARCHIE ROBERTS

"THE BOYS WHO BOMBED BERLIN"
Aircrew from 38 Squadron and 115 Squadron who took part in the first raid on Berlin on 28th/29th August 1940.

when he visited Adolf). We flew around until we made certain of the target, our new captain is most particular. We had a lucky break – a plane in front of us dropped a flare and lit up the target for us, everything was very distinct. We turned round and went in to attack. We let go seven high explosive bombs and a canister of incendiaries. It was our most successful raid so far and without doubt we plastered the target. It was a mass of flames. We saw quite a lot of bomb bursts caused by the other lads taking part and once again all our machines returned safely. On the way back Jerry gave us a lot of hate but it was a 'piece of cake' after the half hour we spent over Berlin."

'P-Peter' landed at 0455 after seven and a half hours in the air. Gunners were told to be alert to the possibility of an attack right up to when the aircraft had landed so Alec waited until they had reached their dispersal before starting his shutting down drill. While there was still power in the

SGT NORMAN STENT

SGT ALEC OLLAR

SGT ALLAN RICHARDSON

SGT CYRIL WESSELS

"THE BOYS WHO BOMBED BERLIN"
These still photographs were taken the day after the raid by the Pathé News crew who filmed the event for the cinemas.

aircraft he rotated the turret to the central position and engaged the locking plunger in the recess of the cam. He then put the 'Fire/Safe' switch to 'Safe', switched off the reflector sight and unloaded the guns by raising the breech cover and pulling back the cocking stud with the loading toggle. He raised the transporter, removed the round from the face of the breech block and, while it was raised, released the end of the belt from the retaining pawl. Finally he pressed down the transporter and closed the breech cover.

Having unplugged his intercom in the prescribed textbook fashion – "Hold the socket in your left hand and withdraw the jack with your right then put the jack in your pocket," he unfastened his safety harness, opened the turret doors in the correct sequence and swung himself out of the turret. Having closed and locked the doors behind him he began his scramble forward and dropped through the crew hatch onto the tarmac below.

After seven and a half hours in the same cramped position. Alec and his fellow crewmen were tired, stiff and hungry and could not wait to return to the Sergeants' Mess for the traditional indulgence reserved for aircrew returning from ops – a bacon and egg breakfast.

A cutting from The Sunday Chronicle. Alec 3rd from left.

The following day the headlines of the national newspapers all told of the first effective raid on Berlin and the bomber crews were the heroes of the hour. Film crews from British Gaumont and Pathé News descended onto the station shooting masses of newsreel footage and stills of the aircraft and their crews who had to get into their flying gear for the shoot:

"If you go to the pictures on Monday, or any time next week, you will probably see me on the screen. They also took some stills and I am in those too. You should get a good view of Archie, he is right in front with a lucky horseshoe mascot."

The Berlin correspondent of the Swedish newspaper *Aftonbladet* reported that the most effective bombing had been in East Berlin where the Goerlitzer railway goods yard at Weinerstrasse, 'the Liverpool Street of Berlin', was set ablaze. This was Sergeant Stent's target and is a fine testimonial to his skill and determination. It was also reported that the success of the raid had led to a burst of fury against Britain in the German press with headlines including: *'Murder'*, *'Shameful, Cowardly Act' and 'Systematic Churchill Manoeuvre to place German Population under Murderous Terror'*. Photographs showed Berliners cursing Britain from the safety of their shelters.

It was the first, but by no means the last, trip that Alec would have to Berlin but their first two operations in September were of an entirely different nature. On 3rd and 6th they were despatched to the Harz Mountains to 'Razzle'. This was to set fire to large tracts of forest, or crops, using unpleasant, little phosphorus-based incendiary devices transported in the aircraft in tanks of water. They were very unstable and it was not unknown for a bomb aimer, whose duty it was to drop them through a hatch in the bottom of the aircraft, to lose two or three fingers due to early ignition nor for a German boy on the ground to pick one up and burn himself very seriously due to late ignition. They were not popular with the crews who had to handle them, nor were they very effective, and their use was eventually discontinued.

❧◌ℰℰ

Another publicity still from Pathé News of aircrew who took part in the first raid on Berlin. Alec can be seen third from right.

Chapter 5 – "Two Birds dead in the Air"

On 9th September they were back to conventional bombing; the target was originally to have been Berlin but this had to be aborted due to weather and the marshalling yards at Brussels were successfully attacked instead. On 14th they were part of a big raid on the *Luftwaffe* French Headquarters in the *Chateau Argentenville* at Nivelles. Two aircraft registered near misses though there was 10/10 cloud cover. On 17th at Ehrang, a German airfield not far from the Luxembourg border, Sergeant Stent again demonstrated his accuracy and resolve when he dropped down to 1,500 feet and dropped two sticks across the target causing explosions and a violent fire.

This was at the time that Hitler was threatening Britain with invasion and was amassing huge fleets of barges in Calais and Ostend for the purpose. On 20th September a force of 45 bombers from Marham and Feltwell crossed the Channel to reduce their numbers. At Calais there was intense searchlight activity and flak and on their first pass it was impossible to sight the target with any accuracy. For the second pass Sergeant Stent dived down from 6,000 to 2,000 feet and in spite of constant attention from the ground defences, plastered the docks with bombs which caused several explosions and lit up the area for the third and final attack. In view of the opposition, this was made from 10,000 feet and many hits were obtained on the now well illuminated target. The intense flak followed the bombers out to sea as they headed for home and it was thought that there may have been a flak ship moored just offshore to see them on their way. Two aircraft were damaged but, remarkably, none was lost.

Two days later they did the same at Le Havre where there was another concentration of invasion barges. Again there was heavy flak but extensive damage was done to the *Basin Manche* and *Basin Leopold* and many barges were destroyed. On the return flight one aircraft had to make a forced landing at Ford due to flak damage but the others got back safely.

On 24th September, Cyril Wessels who was Alec's room mate, was told that from the next operation he was to be given a command of his own. Alec had grown very fond of the quiet little Yorkshireman who was only

21 years of age and, while delighted that he should receive what amounted to a promotion, he would nevertheless miss his calm, reliable presence on operations as would the rest of the crew. The next operation was to be on the 30th and Wessels was to fly 'F-Freddie' 3292 with Sergeants MacNair, Thompson, Pennington, Pritchard and Cameron as his crew.

On the evening of the 30th Alec in 'P-Peter 9285' took off from Marham at 1852 bound for Berlin again. Cyril Wessels followed at 1937 with a less onerous task for his first assignment. Together with Pilot Officer Steel in 'T-Tear 2549' he was sent to attack the marshalling yards at Osnabrück.

The *nachtjagd* unit which Helmut Lent was to join as *Staffelkapitan* the next day, 6./NJG 1 was stationed at Deelen in Holland. North-east of here on the *nachtjagd* defensive line was 2./NJG 1 at Vechta where the *Staffelkapitan* was *Oberleutnant* Werner Streib who had already accounted for four British bombers. At about 2130 on the 30th he was patrolling in his *Zerstorer* when he sighted a group of aircraft and, having identified them as Wellingtons on their way home after bombing Osnabrück, he closed in for the attack. He approached fast on the flank of the first when it was over the village of Badbergen and struck it with a deadly burst from his cannons before he had even been seen; it burst into flames and fell towards the ground in a fireball. Turning hard to port he came round in a full circle and approached the next nearest Wellington.

This time he was spotted and the pilot threw his aircraft into a sharp dive but Streib was sufficiently far off to alter course and take a steady aim.

He shot his victim down over the village of Menslage two minutes after he had destroyed the first. His first victim was Cyril Wessels who was killed with his whole crew.

Hauptmann Werner Streib who became one of Germany's most successful nightfighter pilots

The second of Streib's victims was Pilot Officer Steel who managed to crash land his disabled aircraft. He was captured and spent the rest of the war in a Prisoner-of-War Camp. Streib shot down a third bomber that night which was probably a Whitley or a Wellington from another squadron but was never positively identified.

Apart from the usual flak as they crossed the Dutch coast, 'P-Peter's' flight to Berlin was fairly uneventful but when they reached the outskirts of the city it was clear that the German defences were very much better organised than they had been last time. Batteries of searchlights and heavy flak assailed the bombers as they sought through gaps in the cloud to ascertain their position and identify their target. This was the *Reichsluftfahrt-Ministerium*, the German Air Ministry on the *Leipziger Strasse* south of the River *Spree* in the centre of the city. Last time they were over Berlin they had easily identified the famous *Unter den Linden* by its row of lights and as this ran parallel to the *Leipziger Strasse* they would have had no difficulty in pinpointing it. But the Berliners had learned their lesson and imposed a strict blackout so there was not a guiding light to be seen.

Armstrong Whitworth Whitley Bomber c1940.

RAF OFFICIAL PHOTOGRAPHER

Marham, September 1940.
Back row: **Sergeants Woor, Forrester** (replaced Wessels) **and Stent.**
Front row: **Sergeants Ollar, Peters and Palmer.**

Norman Stent with his passion for accuracy was far from happy; they had identified what they thought was the configuration of the river which fixed their north-south line and from here they would have to estimate the distance due south from the river to the target. This they knew to be about three-quarters of a mile but at the point where they estimated the target should be there was heavy cloud cover. Stent came round again praying for a break in the cloud which would permit a positive identification but by the time they crossed the river again the cloud, if anything, was even thicker than before. It was likely to deteriorate further so there were only two options: to return with their bombs or drop them where they believed the target to be; they chose the latter and as their load fell a very slight gap in the cloud opened to show a straight avenue with a large building which, they told themselves without much confidence, might have been the Air Ministry.

As they climbed away from the city centre Sergeant Woor calculated a course for home but when they approached the outskirts of the city the flak suddenly stopped. They knew with apprehension what this meant: the nightfighters would soon be amongst them. A blazing aircraft falling to earth some distance away on their starboard quarter told of the fate of one of their number; then another closer to them, which looked like a Wellington, was diving steeply with smoke pouring from a burning wing. There was no sign of the crew jumping and they prayed that the pilot might manage to make an intact crash landing – unlikely as that was.

The pilot in the cockpit of a Messerschmitt bf110 (taken from the Funker's seat).

Alec, 100% alert in the rear turret, spotted two aircraft some distance away cutting across 'P-Peter's' trail from left to right. As they banked to starboard he saw their two engines and identified them as bf110s. They were coming round in a curve to attack them on the starboard beam.

"Skipper: stand by for a violent turn left" he told the pilot urgently through the intercom and the pilot acknowledged. He had flown on so many operations with Alec and had complete confidence in his judgement. The other members of the crew knew that they were about to be in close-quarter action and said a silent prayer that they, too, would not be falling to earth in a blazing ball within the next few minutes.

"HARD LEFT NOW," Alec barked and Norman Stent flung the aircraft into a tight turn to port. This was a manoeuvre that the pilot of the leading fighter had not expected; he had been prepared for his victim to drop into a 'corkscrew' dive which was the usual escape tactic. As he readjusted his mind to the new circumstances, his windscreen shattered and he was hit squarely in the face by a stream of fire from his target. As the first attacker dropped away the pilot of the second fighter, now too close for an effective attack, decided to come round again. As he banked away he exposed his under belly to Alec who, with the calm and confidence of a man who, on the moor, was well accustomed to having two birds dead in the air, sent a controlled stream of deadly fire into the underside of his attacker's fuselage. Sergeant Palmer in the starboard beam position, and waiting his opportunity to contribute, saw flames coming from the victim and a piece fly off its tail.

Palmer did not have to wait long for his share of the action; a third bf110 came in tentatively on the starboard beam and was met by a well directed stream of fire from the Wellington's beam position. The German pilot either thought better of it or spotted an easier prey; he dived away and was not seen again. Minutes later Alec saw another bomber on fire to port which he thought might well have been the victim of their last visitor.

The remainder of the flight home was uneventful and they landed back at Marham at 0227 after seven and a half hours in the air. It had been a busy but ultimately disappointing operation: they had no confidence that they had hit the target and they could not claim either of their Messerschmitts as kills as they had not actually seen them destroyed.

Several of the other crews thought they might have hit the target but, like 'P-Peter' none had much confidence.

Thirty-five bombers attacked Berlin that night of which four were lost, two Wellingtons and two Whitleys. Later analysis showed that no bombs had hit the Air Ministry; in fact only six bombs had landed in Berlin that night and most of these were in the western suburbs miles away from the target. It is probable that 'P-Peter' identified the wrong bend in the river and were, in fact, much farther west than they thought and with the heavy cloud it was impossible to confirm their position.

Alec was shocked and saddened the next morning to learn that Cyril Wessels had failed to return. Later in the day the station staff officer came to collect his personal effects, such as they were, for return to his next-of-kin. Alec asked him if he might have the address of Cyril's parents so he might write to them. The officer said yes, of course, but he did realise that the CO would write as a matter of course. Alec knew this but sat down just the same and wrote a long letter to Hermann and Gertrude Wessels which they no doubt treasured for the rest of their lives. Cyril's remains and those of his co-pilot, Sergeant Neville Thompson, and one of his gunners, Sergeant Alexander Cameron were recovered and today lie side by side in the Reichswald Forest War Cemetery. The bodies of Sergeants MacNair, Pennington and Pritchard were never found.

As October progressed the nights lengthened and the weather deteriorated making the task of locating targets even more difficult than previously. Alec flew on operations on 11th, 13th and 15th October and it was only the last of these that resulted in any significant damage. The main target was the *Gneisnau* in Kiel and although the ship could not be found, they managed to cause some fires in the docks area and shipbuilding yards.

On 20th, twelve aircraft from each squadron at Marham were despatched in search of the *Bismarck* which was reported to be in the Blohm and Voss shipyard in Hamburg. The story was much the same as on 15th – bad weather prevented them from finding the ship but they plastered the Hamburg docks with incendiaries and high explosive which was seen to do considerable damage. This was the last operational flight they would do with Norman Stent; he had completed his tour and was posted on 27th to No. 2 School of Air Navigation at Cranage near Crewe. This school had only just opened to offer advanced training to experienced pilots and navigators in celestial navigation. Sergeant Forrester, who had been their second pilot since Cyril Wessel's death, became captain and Sergeant Rawlings joined the crew as second pilot.

On the way to bomb Gelsenkirchen on 27th, Pilot Officer Rodger's plane which was flying with them, developed engine trouble over the Dutch coast. The starboard engine then stopped completely and they had to turn round and try to struggle home on one engine. They could not quite make it and crashed at Oulton in Yorkshire; they all suffered broken bones.

The following day the squadron was ordered to send three aircraft with their crews to Malta and for 20 maintenance crews to follow by sea. The detachment was under the command of Squadron Leader Foss and the three aircraft captains were Pilot Officer Pate and Sergeant Dyer, both of whom had flown beside them on many missions, and their own pilot Sergeant Forrester. They departed the next day on 29th and on 30th Pate and his entire crew were killed when they flew into a balloon cable over Iver in Buckinghamshire. Sergeant Forrester had to return to Marham with technical problems. Their old navigator, Sergeant Thomas Woor, also went with the Malta contingent and was killed together with Philip Forrester five days later.

With his old crew broken up and dispersed, Alec was now assigned to a new crew. Among them he was delighted to see his old friend Cecil May with whom he had gone through training. Cecil, as well as being a trained Air Gunner, was also qualified as a wireless operator.

The aircraft captain was Pilot Officer Charles Petley who

Sergeant Cecil May.

Marham, October 1940.
From left: **Sergeants Ollar and Davidson; Pilot Officers Petley and Currie; Sergeants Munby and May.**

was a Cambridge Double First and came from a distinguished family which could trace its origins as Scottish landowners back to the 17th century. The second pilot was Pilot Officer Curry; the navigator Sergeant Munby; the wireless operator Sergeant Davidson and Sergeant Cecil May was acting as forward gunner though trained in two roles. Alec joined them on 16th November, as a last minute replacement for Sergeant Bennett, just before take-off, .

It was a bad trip. A force of 130 aircraft, 11 of which were from 115 Squadron, were sent to bomb Hamburg but had to divert to their secondary targets because of 10/10 cloud cover. Alec's plane bombed nearby Emden with moderate success. The force had been beset with heavy flak but as they turned for home the nightfighters were upon them and exacted a heavy toll: of the eleven 115 Squadron aircraft, two, flown by Sergeants Larkman and English, were shot down. Three others, flown by Pilot Officers Tindall and Roy and Flight Lieutenant Van, were badly mauled. Van, though his aircraft was badly damaged, managed to limp back to Marham; Roy got to England but crashed at Wittering his crew suffering only minor injuries; Tindall, with great skill, managed to extricate himself from a determined attack by four bf110s which caused extensive damage to his aircraft and seriously wounded the front gunner, 20 year-old Sergeant Frederick Jervis.

While Tindall and his second pilot, Sergeant Hartland struggled to fly the badly damaged plane home, Flight Sergeant Bryant, the navigator, and Sergeant Howard, the wireless operator, did what they could to dress Jervis's wounds and make him comfortable. Pilot Officer Hinxman, the rear gunner, remained on guard in his turret lest they should come under renewed attack from fighters.

They could not quite reach home and had to make a forced landing at RAF Bircham Newton in Norfolk. As soon as the aircraft had come to a standstill an ambulance arrived and Sergeant Jervis was taken for medical attention but his injuries were too grievous and he died within hours. At his parents' request he was buried in his home village of Barwell in Leicestershire.

In the Merignac suburb of Bordeaux is an aircraft factory which today is the Dassault Mirage plant. In 1940 it was being used by the Germans to produce their Focke-Wulf Fw189 *Uhu* 'Eagle Owl'. This was a twin-engined, twin boom, highly manoeuvrable reconnaissance machine used extensively in support of the Wehrmacht; it was known as 'the eyes of the army'. This factory was to be the next target for Pilot Officer Petley and his crew together with another two Wellingtons from 115 Squadron flown by Sergeant Marriott and Pilot Officer Bois. It was a very long flight and the crews were to be in the air for nine hours.

The route had to be carefully chosen to avoid the heavily defended German naval bases on the Biscay coast – Brest, Lorient and Saint-Nazaire. The bombers took off from Marham just after midnight on 22nd November and had an untroubled flight across the north-west corner of France crossing the coast north of La Rochelle then feeling their way along the coast until they located the Gironde Estuary. Once again, the quickest and most certain way of finding their target would be by following the course of the river until the centre of the city of Bordeaux then crossing the city and flying due west for six miles from the river.

Marham 1940. Three of Alec's friends from 38 Squadron which was 125's sister squadron at Marham. *From left:* **Sergeants Archie Roberts, Allan Richardson and Jimmy Somerville**

The Gironde Estuary is about three miles wide where it meets the sea but they recognised it without too much difficulty then started their journey up river which, in more pacific times, would have been a claret-lover's dream as they passed the great estates of Bordeaux on either bank – Medoc, Pauillac and Margaux to starboard and the *Cote de Blaye* to port. There was a fork in the river just beyond Bayonne-sur-Gironde and they were careful to follow the right hand stream which would lead them to the city of Bordeaux. There was a loop in the river at the *Quai des Queyries* on the east bank from where they should be able to see a great bridge, the *Pont Pierre,* with eighteen arches. At this point they should turn west.

Visibility, for a change, was excellent. They identified the *Pont Pierre* from far away, turned west at the *Quai des Queyries*, flew for six miles and there were the runways and hangars of the factory. It was a rare occasion when everything went entirely to plan; for once they could see their target clearly and plastered the hangars and factory buildings with high explosives and incendiaries. Before they turned for home they had the satisfaction of seeing, and photographing, the blazing buildings below. There had been a little, not very effective, anti-aircraft ground fire but it was nothing compared with the intense and accurate fire they were accustomed to in the German homeland. Their long return flight was without incident and they landed at Marham at 0900. There had been no casualties.

Two days later Alec was on operations again having been attached to another crew. His new captain was an Australian, Squadron Leader Mulholland, with Sergeants Molony, second pilot; Symons, navigator; Williamson, wireless operator and Sutherland, front gunner. Alec's friend Cecil May took his place in Pilot Officer Tetley's crew. Eight aircraft from 115 Squadron were part of a 42-aircraft force tasked to bomb Hamburg. The city was obscured by cloud but they bombed just the same. Two aircraft from the formation were lost but neither was from Marham.

And so it was that on 27th November Alec, now as rear gunner in Squadron Leader Mulholland's crew, took part in the raid over Cologne and met the King on his return.

„Heim ins Reich!"...

Hunderttausende deutscher Familien sehnen sich zur Weihnachtszeit nach der Heimkehr ihrer Väter, Söhne und Brüder.

„Heim ins Reich!" Diese Worte habt Ihr oft genug von Euren Naziführern gehört. Nach ihren Beteuerungen wollten sie ja eigentlich nichts anderes als die „unglücklichen Auslandsdeutschen" heim ins Reich zu führen. Um das zu erreichen, so sagten sie Euch, mußte Deutschland in diesen Krieg ziehen.

Heute sind die deutschen Soldaten selber die Auslandsdeutschen. Wie der ewige Jude werden sie von Euren Führern von Land zu Land gejagt. Infolge des unersättlichen Machthungers Eurer Führer muß heute der deutsche Soldat seine Weihnachten in trüber Einsamkeit, fern von der Heimat verbringen, von allen gemieden, überall gehaßt.

Und nicht nur Eure Soldaten werden von Heimat und Familie ferngehalten. Hunderttausende deutscher Arbeiter und Bauern werden heute hin und hertransportiert wie das dumpfe Vieh. Der Willkür der Naziführer ausgeliefert, müssen sie nach Polen, nach der Tschechoslovakei, nach Österreich; niemand fragt sie, ob sie wollen oder nicht.

Wann gibt's denn endlich eine Heimkehr ins Reich für all diese Männer, Brüder und Söhne?! Es gibt eben keine Heimkehr, solange das Naziregime besteht. Solange die Raubordnung Europas noch dauert, wird sie stets von deutschen Bajonetten aufgezwungen und durch das Schuften der heutigen unfreiwilligen „Auslandsdeutschen" aufrechterhalten werden müssen. Darum müssen Eure Lieben diese Weihnachten weit weg von Euch verbringen. Und darum werden sie auch in der Fremde bleiben müssen, bis wir Europa befreit haben.

459

FRIEDE AUF ERDEN – DAFÜR KÄMPFEN ENGLAND UND SEINE VERBÜNDETEN!

"Return to the Reich!"

German families in their hundreds of thousands are longing for their fathers, sons and brothers to return home for Christmas.

"Return to the Reich!" You've heard your Nazi leaders say these words many times. They have been assuring you that bringing the "hapless German expatriates" back into the Reich was all they wanted. To this aim, so they keep telling you, Germany had to wage this war.

Today, the German soldiers are themselves "hapless German expatriates". Like the eternally migrating Wandering Jew, they are hunted by your leaders from one country to the next. It is because of your leaders' insatiable appetite for power that the German soldier has to spend Christmas in solitude, far away from home, shunned by everybody, hated everywhere.

But not only your soldiers are kept far away from their homes and families. Hundreds of thousands of German workers and farmers are being ferried around these days like cattle. Under the despotic rule of the Nazi leaders they have to go to Poland, Czechoslovakia, Austria; they are not asked whether they want to go.

When will these men, brothers and sons finally be allowed to return home to the Reich? As long as the Nazi regime stays in power, there will be no return for them. As long as the marauding of Europe continues, it will always be enforced by German bayonets and will always have to be kept alive by the hard labour of today's involuntary "German expatriates". This is the reason why your loved ones will spend this Christmas far away from you. And this is the reason why they will be staying in foreign countries, until we will have liberated Europe.

"I wish it was already over!" The only consolation for every German is the thought of peace in the near future. Today, you are praying for victory over England and her allies. We know that you don't lust for any more victories; you have had enough of all your victories. You know very well that they only have temporary meaning in practical terms. But you have been told over and over again: "one more victory is all we need", then there will be peace.

A victory gained by Nazi Germany will not bring peace. Your masters' hunger for power and delusions of grandeur know no boundaries. Every new victory would only be a prelude to further wars.

There is only one way to bring about peace: The masters of the German war machinery have to disappear, once and for all, only then can there be peace again on earth.

This is what England is fighting for, this is what her allies are fighting for. It is the duty of every German man, every German woman, to join our fighters, if they really want peace on earth.

Peace on earth – This is what England and her allies are fighting for!

An example of the type of propaganda leaflets dropped over Germany by Bomber Command in operations known as "Gardening".

Chapter 6 – Instructor

During 1940, after Britain's defeat in France and humiliation at Dunkirk, the only aggressive actions which Britain or her allies had been able to take against Germany in Europe were the raids undertaken by Bomber Command. The fighters had certainly performed with valour during the Battle of Britain but this was in the defensive role. Fighters were defenders, bombers were attackers. So it was that, after the *Luftwaffe's* failure to bring Britain to her knees during the summer of 1940, and Hitler's indefinite postponement, or perhaps abandonment, of his invasion plans, the Germans' top priority became the development of the fighter units which would protect the fatherland; in particular the nightfighters which were already proving themselves highly effective predators among the bomber formations.

In September Germany, Italy and Japan entered a 'Tripartite Pact', an agreement for mutual assistance, and the 'Axis' was born. The USSR was invited to join and Hitler, now confident of victory, offered them India as their share of the spoils. But the Soviets wanted more than this and, before the year was out, the Axis powers were secretly planning for the two most elemental, and ultimately disastrous, acts of aggression of the war – the invasion of Russia by Germany and the attack on Pearl Harbour by Japan.

Germany, meanwhile, continued to bomb ostensibly industrial and military targets in Britain but in November they started large-scale indiscriminate bombing of city centres; a blitz on Southampton was followed by a massive attack on Coventry which would establish the technique needed to cause maximum destruction of buildings and would challenge the hitherto moral restrictions on bombing in civilian areas. A force of 515 German bombers attacked the city for nearly 12 hours, arriving around 7 pm on the 14th and the final all-clear sounding at 6.15 the following morning; 4,300 homes were destroyed and around two-thirds of the city's public buildings were damaged including hospitals and churches and, of course, the ancient cathedral; 568 civilians were killed. The first waves of aircraft dropped high explosive bombs which broke through roofs

The ruins of Coventry Cathedral on 16th November 1940, two days after the Luftwaffe's raid which killed 568 civilians and destroyed 4,300 homes.

and opened up buildings for the subsequent deluge of incendiaries. This technique would later be adopted by both sides. Some 500 tonnes of high explosive bombs and 36,000 incendiaries were dropped.

Churchill decided that a retaliatory raid should be mounted to demonstrate that Britain was no longer prepared to be constrained by a moral code which was palpably being disregarded by Germany. On 16th December Alec, still part of Squadron Leader Mulholland's crew, took off for Mannheim on what would prove to be Bomber Command's most consequential raid so far and one which would herald a fundamental change in its strategy. This was the first raid by the RAF on other than specific military or industrial targets and was its start of what would later be known as 'Area Bombing'.

Eight Wellingtons from 115 Squadron were part of a force of 134 aircraft comprising the largest formation of bombers so far sent on a single operation. Despite good visibility and a full moon, results were not spectacular; the city centre, which was the primary target, was largely missed with the majority of the damage being done in the residential suburbs; 476 buildings were destroyed and 33 civilians were killed (compared with 568 in the *Luftwaffe* raid on Coventry). Ground defensive fire was light and only three aircraft from the entire force were lost although several subsequently crashed or made forced landings in England. In sixteen months of warfare, very little progress had been made in target location and bombing accuracy both of which were largely dependent on visual recognition which in turn was governed by weather conditions.

On the Mannheim raid an early use of a 'pathfinder' force was tried out with eight Wellingtons, with experienced crews, going ahead of the main force to identify the target and mark it with incendiaries. However, they failed to identify the city centre which thereby escaped the attention of the following force. Although research on electronic navigation was in progress, the advantages of *Gee, Oboe* and *H2S* were still to come. In 1940 it was estimated that only one in ten bombs hit their primary target.

Alec made the last operational flight of his first tour on 22nd December 1940; the target was the wharves on the River Scheldt at Vissingen in Holland, known to the British as Flushing. It was also his last operational flight with Norman Mulholland who, to the delight of his crew had just been awarded the DFC (Distinguished Flying Cross). It was a straightforward operation without major incident, taking off at 1748 and returning to Marham at 2105, in time to get a good night's sleep for a change.

A normal tour of duty was for 30 operations and Alec, having now completed 34, was due for a posting. Earlier in the year his Squadron Commander had tried to persuade him to put in for a commission but Alec had declined. Now the subject was raised again – he had completed a full operational tour and proved himself a very competent gunner and, being somewhat older than the average crewman, tended to be something of a father figure to his younger fellows who often turned to him for counsel on personal as well as service matters. He was ideal officer material, his CO told him; but he had not changed his mind.

The difference between commissioned and non-commissioned ranks in the RAF was very different from the other two services. Being a young service, the Air Force was not constrained by the traditions and

**Advanced Gunnery Refresher Course, RAF Stradishall, February 1941.
Alec is third from right front row.**

prejudices which had established themselves over hundreds of years within the Navy and the Army; there was no class barrier between officers and men in the Air Force, with the majority of officers, then as now, tending to come from grammar rather than public schools, and it was not the practice in the RAF to post a newly-commissioned officer to a different unit to separate him from his previous circle of friends and workmates; he simply continued doing the same job he had been doing previously with a few more privileges and a bit more pay. Alec was very comfortable in the relaxed fellowship of the Sergeants' Mess and had no wish to make the transition. He was therefore posted to Stradishall, Suffolk, on an advanced gunnery refresher course to qualify as an instructor

The course consisted of fairly intensive air to ground and air to air firing and evaluation with theoretical updating between flying days. All the students on the course were experienced gunners who had completed a full tour of operations and the nine men in Alec's squad had all accounted for enemy aircraft. A B Austin, Air Correspondent of *The Daily Herald* visited the course and the following extract appeared as part of his article in the 12th February edition:

> **"I have just watched nine young men preparing for the next Blitz on Germany. They are nine out of many thousands of air gunners who are going back to school in**

9 YOUNG MEN
are training others for our new Blitz in Hitler's skies

● by
A. B. AUSTIN
Air Correspondent

I HAVE just watched nine young men preparing for the next Blitz on Germany.

They are nine out of many thousands of air gunners who are going back to school in the skies in order that aim and touch and timing may be perfect when the moment comes.

THE NIGHT BOMBER GUNNER FIRES HIS GUNS PERHAPS ONCE IN THIRTY RAIDS. IF HE DOESN'T HIT HIS MESSERSCHMITT THAT ONCE, HE WILL PROBABLY LOSE HIS OWN LIFE AND THE LIVES OF FIVE, SIX OR SEVEN OTHER MEN.

Whatever the effect of a new Blitz on Germany, the future strength and staying power of the R A F depend on the patience, quickness and aim of its air gunners.

That is why the nine young men, and many others like them, are putting all air gunners through a hard refresher course, letting them shoot all over the skies above a lonely patch of England, making them fire their film-camera guns at our own fighters and then come back and criticise their own gunnery on the screen.

VETERANS ALL

I choose the nine young men because they are veterans of the air war. Between them they have been everywhere that a bomber can go from England.

They saw the towns of Holland and Belgium ablaze from the Zuyder Zee to the Straits of Dover ("Most horrible sight of the war").

They bombed Italy and flew over Mont Blanc in the moonlight.

They took their patience and their tireless eyes to Norway and

timing. He is the man who orders the 'evasive action.' He has got to make the hare jink just when the greyhound is going to bite."

The nine young men are all Flight-Sergeants. Eight of them have the D.F.M., and the D.F.M. on a sergeant gunner's tunic usually means far greater endurance and many more hours of flying against the enemy than the D.F.C. on a fighter pilot's tunic.

"GINGER" & JOCK

"Ginger," for instance, most experienced of the nine, has flown on 66 raids, all of them in the same squadron of Wellingtons, and all of them over enemy territory.

I doubt if any air gunner has a better record. His friend Jock has flown on 95 raids, but most of them have been with Coastal Command over waters where flak and Messerschmitts are not so plentiful.

"Ginger" is in his early twenties, a reddish haired, grinning Londoner. He is unmarried. They say air gunners are better unmarried. The only domestic scene in "Ginger's" career was when they had to force him to part with his squadron and take a rest.

And the only mistake he has ever made in the air was when he identified a pheasant as a pigeon.

* * *

Jock, a quiet, dependable motor mechanic from Berwick-on-Tweed, has the penetrating light blue eyes

'A lot depends on the air gunner

Scots: Alec from Edinburgh; Geordie, with his black hair and his reddish, grinning face, from Stirling.

They were together in a bomber with an Australian pilot who could not understand a word they said. An English gunnery officer translated for them.

* * *

✝ Alec, the pale-faced, thoughtful type of Scot, has shot down two German fighters from his Wellington. He was in the very first raid on Berlin.

the skies in order that aim and touch and timing may be perfect when the moment comes.

"The night bomber gunner fires his guns perhaps once in thirty raids. If he doesn't hit his Messerschmitt that once he will probably lose his own life and the lives of five, six or seven other men.

"Whatever the effect of a new Blitz on Germany, the future strength and staying power of the RAF depends on the patience, quickness and aim of its air gunners. That is why the nine young men, and many others like them, are putting all air gunners through a hard refresher course, letting them shoot all over the skies above a lonely patch of England, making them fire their film-camera guns at our own fighters and then come back and criticise their own gunnery on the screen.

"I choose the nine young men because they are veterans of the air war. Between them they have been everywhere that a bomber can go from England. They saw the towns of Holland and Belgium ablaze from the Zuyder Zee to the Straits of Dover ('Most horrible sight of the war').

"They bombed Italy and flew over Mont Blanc in the moonlight. They took their patience and their tireless eyes to Norway and the Atlantic, to the Ruhr, to Hamburg and Bremen, to Brest and Berlin.

"If you lumped them together you would find all the qualities that go to make the perfect air gunner. A gunnery officer gave me a word picture of this paragon:

'He is very robust. That's his first quality, otherwise he couldn't stick ten hours in a cold, cramped tail turret.

'He can stand any amount of solitude. Countrymen make the best tail gunners, though they don't train so quickly.

'He is patient and thorough. Ninety percent of his job is not shooting, but searching the sky.

'He has a calm, steady voice. To the crew the tail gunner

**is only a voice, the voice that tells the pilot how to turn
when an enemy attacks from the rear.**

**'He has a perfect sense of timing. He is the man who
orders the evasive action. He has got to make the hare jink
just when the greyhound is going to bite.'**

**"The nine young men are all Flight-Sergeants. Eight of
them have the DFM and the DFM on a Sergeant Gunner's
tunic usually means far greater endurance and many more
hours of flying than the DFC on a fighter pilot's tunic."**

Squadron Leader Norman Mulholland finished his first tour at the same
time as Alec and took over command of No.3 Group Training Flight at
Stradishall to which Alec was next posted as an instructor. On 24th February
Mulholland was promoted to Wing Commander and on 7th March Alec
learned that he had been awarded the Distinguished Flying Medal for
"gallantry and devotion to duty in the execution of air operations." On 1st
April he was promoted to Flight Sergeant and gained a crown above his
Sergeant's stripes and four days later he travelled to London where His
Majesty the King presented his award at an Investiture at Buckingham
Palace. Though the King met thousands of his servicemen and women in
the course of a year, he remembered Alec from their meeting at Marham
after the Cologne raid and mentioned their shared interest in shooting.

During his time with No.3 Group Training Flight at Stradishall,
Alec and his fellow instructors were again featured in several articles in
newspapers and magazines. On 1st March 1941 *Picture Post* carried an
article by A F Shaw which included the following description of the air
gunner's role:

**"Upon the ability of the air gunner, his skill in handling the
guns, his steadiness of nerve, hands and eyes depends the
lives of five other men and an aircraft which cost £30,000
or so to build. It may be a raid on Berlin, a nine-hour trip,
or on Venice which is a ten- or eleven-hour journey. It may
be a short run to Mannheim or Bremen, a mere seven
hours, but throughout all this time, from the take-off to the**

POSTAGRAM. Originator's Reference Number:—

To: SGT. A.J.S. Oller, D.F.M.
      115, Squadron,
      Marham.

Date:— March 8th. 1941.

From: A.O.C.   No 3 Group.

Heartiest congratulations on His Majesty's award

of Distinguished Flying Medal.

Buckingham Palace. 2219

Admit one to witness the Investiture.

- 5 APR 1941

Lord Chamberlain.

Originator's
Signature

P.A. to A.O.C.,

---

landing, the air gunner sits on a small leather seat – just made to fit – in a small turret which gives him no room to stretch. In icy temperatures, degrees below zero, he sits there, slowly swinging his turret round, keeping a watch for enemy fighters and anything else which proves interesting and of assistance to the pilot. Constantly on the alert, fingers resting on the triggers which are seldom used, he dare not relax.

"Perhaps this is not most people's idea of a pleasant job, but it has to be done. There is no pattern among the air gunners, they are of all ages from 20 to over 40; they are of all types. At one bomber station alone I met a gold prospector, a racehorse trainer, a professional boxer, a civil servant, a vacuum cleaner salesman, a journalist and a grocer.

Picture Post,
March 1, 1941

POST

A feature on air
gunners in Picture
Post on 1st March
1941 showed Alec
(left foreground) **with
other gunners
cleaning their guns.
The caption is
headed: "The guns
he takes a pride in".**

. . . "So you see the general run of things with the air
gunner is cold and cramp, watch and ward, little
excitement in shooting and shouting. But the air gunner is
there when he is wanted. he knows the risks he runs, he
knows the chances he takes. He can take it – and give it."

Alec enjoyed his time as an instructor at Stradishall; he found it immensely satisfying to pass on some of his skills to a new generation of young men although, as he told Nessie in a letter in April, it was sad to think that in one year's time half of them would probably be dead. Casualties in Bomber Command were heavy and members of operational crews had to develop a hard veneer on their emotions as, day by day, they never knew which of their friends would fail to return. Theirs was a detached form of warfare which demanded a unique sort of courage: they seldom saw the face of their enemy and could not really afford to think too closely of the damage their own bombs did on the ground. Night after night they had to go to war with the knowledge that this mission might be their last.

A few could not take the strain and were not able to complete their tour. This was Bomber Command's form of shell shock and it received little sympathy from the establishment. As previously mentioned, those who succumbed to the pressure and broke down mentally, were labelled 'LMF', Lacking in Moral Fibre, and were posted away with a black mark on their records.

The King and Queen on a visit to RAF Stradishall in March 1941.

BACK ROW:- SAWYER - NORMAN - HANCOCK- SOPER - MURCH - EAST- MURRAY. JEFFS.
MIDDLE ROW:- DUFREEZ - GOLLD - NICHOLSON - GREENWOOD- SLATFORD - BUTCHER - CUNNINGHAM.
FRONT ROW:- EAGLETON - TOWNDROW - WALKLYN - SGT CRAVEN - F/SGT OLLAR - SGT WOOLBRIDGE - LAMB. PAXTON
        INSTRUCTOR   INSTRUCTOR   INSTRUCTOR   WHITE

Flight-Sergeant Ollar with two of his instructors and some of their trainees.

However, such thoughts were far from the minds of Alec's young trainees who were full of enthusiasm and could not wait to be sitting behind their guns with a German fighter in their sights. They would learn.

One of the pilots in the training flight at Stradishall who became a particular friend of Alec's was Sergeant Max Schonbach. Schonbach was a

Sergeant Max Schonbach. Jewish aircrew were advised to change their names in case they were shot down and captured by the Germans.

Polish jew who had come to Britain in 1931 and become a naturalised British citizen. Anti-semitism was universal throughout Europe in the 1930s and was particularly strong in Poland where a jew stood little chance of admission into the strongly traditional armed services. As Hitler's hatred of the jews became increasingly evident, thousands came to Britain from Germany, Poland and other mid-European countries to avoid persecution. Many of these refugees in Britain volunteered for active service but as anti-semitism, albeit in a much more benign form, was also widespread in Britain, they were initially only accepted in non-combatant roles. This, however, was eventually relaxed and hundreds of jews, like Max Schonbach, volunteered for aircrew training in Bomber Command. These men were particularly brave as they knew that if they were shot down in Europe and captured by the Germans, their chances of survival, as both jews and 'terror bombers', were very thin.

Many were advised to change their names to something less jewish sounding and many did this, including Max Schonbach who was born Michal Bikel, but it is uncertain if this measure actually saved many of these gallant people who were taken as prisoners-of-war.

Instructors at Stradishall.
From left, back row: **Sergeant Avory, Flight-Sergeant Ollar, Sergeant Humm.**
Front row: **Sergeants Ludgate, Jones and Drake.**

Queen Wilhelmina of the Netherlands in 1942. The Dutch were forbidden by the Germans to celebrate her birthday in any way.

UNITED NATIONS INFORMATION OFFICE, NEW YORK

Before the war and before the friendship between Britain and the Netherlands had developed, little love was lost between the two nations. Holland had been one of Britain's traditional enemies in past centuries and, in more recent times, the overseas colonial interests of the two countries had often conflicted. In particular, Britain's annexation of the Transvaal and Orange Free State during the Boer War had caused deep resentment among the Dutch. The early colonists had come from Holland and the Dutch felt a strong protective affection for their descendants. After World War 1, the Kaiser had fled into exile in the Netherlands who refused several applications for his extradition which, in turn, caused considerable ill feeling in Britain.

Nevertheless, when Germany invaded the Netherlands in May 1940, Britain sent a destroyer, HMS *Hereward,* to rescue the Dutch Queen Wilhelmina and her family and give them sanctuary in Britain from where she could establish a Dutch Government in Exile. A special radio station, *Radio Oranj*, was allowed to broadcast from BBC transmitters to the Dutch people; Queen Wilhelmina spoke to them regularly and did much to keep up the spirits of her defeated subjects.

The Queen in Exile became a focus for the Dutch nation and the Germans, anxious to challenge her influence, forbade any celebration of her birthday on 31st August, a prohibition which was largely ignored by the Dutch who covertly gathered together to sing the national anthem and crouched secretly over illegal radios to hear the queen's broadcast. At Queen Wilhelmina's request, the RAF agreed to deliver her own contribution to the birthday celebrations.

This would consist of an air drop of cigarettes specially made with tobacco from the Dutch East Indies with the Queen's crown, cypher and birthday date on the front of each packet. The back carried the slogan *Nederland zal herrijzen!* – The Netherlands will rise again! A pattern of 'Vs' for Victory on a dutch orange background completed the design. Also included in the drop were packets of tea and sweets.

Queen Wilhelmina's birthday gift of cigarettes to the Dutch people.
Nederland zal herrijzen! – **The Netherlands will rise again!**

This historic photograph shows the "special" crew selected to deliver Queen Wilhelmina's birthday gift to the Dutch people on 31st August 1941.

From left: **Sergeant W Wooldridge** *(wireless operator)*; **Squadron Leader M T Stephens** *(front gunner)*; **Squadron Leader P C Pickard** *(second pilot)*; **Flight Lieutenant T C McGillivray** *(pilot)*; **Squadron Leader A G S Cousens** *(navigator)*; **Flight Sergeant A J S Ollar** *(rear gunner)*.

Norman Mulholland had been succeeded as Commanding Officer of No. 3 Group Training Flight by Squadron Leader M T Stephens DFC, RAFVR an air gunner with whom Alec found an immediate rapport as they were both shooting men in civilian life. Before he had joined up, Martin Stephens had been a much respected Shooting Editor of *The Field*. Now, as CO of the Training Flight, he was tasked with selecting a high-calibre crew and arranging the flight to deliver Queen Wilhelmina's birthday gifts.

First he selected one of his best and most experienced pilots, Flight Lieutenant Thomas McGillivray a New Zealander of Scots descent from Otago. He had already completed one operational tour and would shortly move to an operational squadron to start his second. An old friend of Stephens, Squadron Leader P C Pickard DSO, DFC, heard of the mission and asked if he could come; Pickard was a well known face as he had played the part of the captain of 'F-Freddie' in *Target for Tonight* a widely distributed semi-documentary following the crew of a Wellington on an operation over Germany. Though he was one of the most experienced and successful bomber pilots in the RAF, he insisted on flying as second pilot on this trip as he did not wish to usurp McGillivray in his own aircraft. For a navigator, Pickard recommended Squadron Leader Alan Cousens DFC who was currently in a staff position at Group Headquarters and was considered one of the best navigators around.

For a rear gunner he could do no better than take his senior instructor, Flight Sergeant Ollar, whom he tasked with selecting the best gunner/wireless operator in the flight. Alec chose one of his most trusted instructors, Sergeant Wilfred Wooldridge who, like everyone else in this select crew, had already completed one operational tour.

Martin Stephens was not going to be left behind himself so, although he was normally a rear gunner, he placed himself in the front turret for this special operation. They took off at 2145 pm in one of the Training Squadron's Wellingtons, No.3202, returning to Marham at 0145 the next morning.There can be little doubt that the mission brought hope and cheer to the Dutch citizens who gathered for clandestine celebrations on their exiled monarch's birthday.

Alec was to be involved in one more goodwill operation over Holland on the night of 9th December 1941.

The principal Christmas celebration in the Netherlands is held on 6th December when, according to their traditions, *Sinterklaas* (Santa Claus or Saint Nicholas) comes to Holland and parades through a Dutch city. When this is Amsterdam he would, in peacetime, visit the queen in her palace. He arrives the night before with his servants, the *Zwaarte Pieten*, Black Peters, who keep a record of which children have been good during the previous year and which have been bad. The children leave out clogs beside the hearth on the night of the 5th and the Black Peters come down the chimney and leave presents in the clogs of the good children. The bad children are put in the Black Peters' sacks and taken to Spain for a year, where *Sinterklaas* lives, to learn how to behave.

If the children leave some hay and carrots in their clog, *Sinterklaas's* horse, who pulls his sleigh over the rooftops during the night, will leave them some sweets in exchange. On the approach to St. Nicholas's Day in 1941, it was decided that the RAF should take over this duty.

It was winter and Bomber Command's activities were very light in view of the weather. On the night of the 5th visibility was down to zero and the operation had to be postponed. It was the same the following night and it was not until the 8th that the weather had lifted sufficiently for the mission to proceed. A scratch crew comprising Sergeant Thompson, Pilot Officer Barrett, Warrant Officer Binns, and Flight Sergeants Whittaker, Brownlow and Ollar took off at 0400 on the morning of the 9th and dropped thousands of packets of Pascall sweets over the Netherlands – a slightly late, but nonetheless very welcome gift from *Sinterklaas*.

The back of the packet shows a Black Peter giving Adolf Hitler a good thrashing with a birch while a terrified Mussolini, his head poking out of Black Peter's bag, awaits his turn. The front of the packets showed St Nicholas with one of his Black Peters flying in an RAF fighter and throwing out sweets for the children *(see opposite)*.

The rest of Alec's time with the Training Flight was fairly routine. In July the flight had moved from Stradishall to Newmarket and in February 1942 it became 1483 Target Towing and Gunnery Flight. The training itinerary was intensive and he would take classes up on most days, sometimes two flights in a day. There were three days off at Christmas with normal training flights on 23rd and then resuming on 27th.

SURPRISE VOOR HITLER

ZIE de maan schijnt door de boomen,
Makker, hoort het wild geraas.
De R.A.F. is weer gekomen,
Die is in de lucht de baas!
Vol verwachting klopt ons hart,
Wie de koek krijgt, wie de gard,
Hitler heeft den strijd gestart,
Maar, aan 't eind krijgt hij de gard!

Afzender: St. Nicolaas,
per adres de R.A.F.

Back of packet:

SURPRISE FOR HITLER

See the moon shining through the trees
Friends, hear the wild roar!
The RAF has returned once more,
To rule the airs, watch how they soar.
Our hearts beat in expectation,
Who gets the cake, who the stick.
Hitler started this confrontation,
But it will be he who gets the stick.

**Sender: St. Nicholas
c/o The RAF**

Side of packet:

PASCALL'S SWEETS

Back of packet:

ST. NICHOLAS'S EVE 1941

RAF Rascal
Throw something in my shoe.
Throw bombs at the Krauts,
But scatter sweets in Holland.

HERE COME THE AIRCRAFT . . .

Here come the aircraft from England again.
Bringing many bombs, Germany bound
Promptly to fall on German soil, which will
Soon be gone should this be prolonged.

**Sender: St. Nicholas
SCATTERED BY THE RAF**

Side of packet (not shown):

**The Netherlands will rise again!
ORANGE WILL TRIUMPH**

STROOIAVOND 1941

R.A.F. Kapoentje,
Gooi wat in mijn schoentje.
Bij de moffen gooien,
Maar in Holland strooien!

ZIE GINDS KOMT . . .

ZIE ginds komt het vliegtuig uit
Engeland weer aan.
Het brengt heel wat bommen, die naar
Duitschland gaa
Die vallen die dadelijk op Mofrika neer,
Is dat lang zoo doorgaat, dan is er niet
veel meer!

Afzender: St. Nicolaas,
per adres de R.A.F.

STROOID DOOR DE R.A.F.

Pilot Officer A J S Ollar, DFM, RAFVR

In March 1942 Alec was told that he was to be commissioned at the end of the month whether he liked it or not and would then be sent back to 115 Squadron to commence his second tour of operations. His protests about the promotion were in vain; on 28th March he made his last flight as a Flight Sergeant and one week later on 2nd April he made his first as a Pilot Officer.

Alec's tour as an instructor finished on 8th April but on 11th he flew again as an Air Gunner in a North Sea search for a missing aircraft. At 1015 on 13th April Pilot Officer A J S Ollar DFM took off as a passenger in Flight Sergeant Stoddart's Wellington on a cross country exercise to Grangemouth from where he travelled home to Edinburgh for two week's leave before taking up his new post with 115 Squadron at Marham.

Chapter 7 – Rise of the Nachtjagd

During the first half of 1941, while Alec was an instructor at Stradishall, the strategic objectives of Britain's bomber offensive had deviated with the developing priorities decided by government. At the start of the year it was thought that Germany's most vulnerable point was her supplies of oil which, experts advised, could reach crisis point by the middle of the year. The bomber force was therefore directed to concentrate its entire attention on the enemy's synthetic oil industry – a campaign which never had much chance of success firstly due to the poor winter weather, secondly the immensity of the task for the limited force of aircraft available and, thirdly, the fact that the morale of the crews was beginning to waiver a bit with the knowledge that the extant technology did little to assist them to improve their performance, the ineffectiveness of which they were becoming increasingly aware.

Meanwhile, having failed to bring Britain to her knees with the attacks on her airfields and the blitz on her capital city, Germany was now concentrating on the blockade of Britain's sea routes. Without imports from America, Britain could not feed her citizens nor satisfy the voracious appetite of her vital rearmament programme. The Atlantic therefore became the battleground where huge escorted convoys of merchant ships, heavily laden with vital supplies, plied constantly back and forth between the New and the Old Worlds.

Germany's three principal weapons in this campaign were, firstly, her U-boats which were being built in large quantities and were now operating from the French Biscay ports of Lorient and St. Nazaire – ideally placed for Atlantic patrols; secondly, her heavily-gunned surface raiders such as the *Gneisenau* and the *Scharnhorst,* against which the lightly-armed Royal Navy escorts would be helpless and, thirdly, her Fokke-Wulf *Condor* long-range reconnaissance and maritime patrol aircraft which Churchill described as 'the scourge of the Atlantic'. These huge, 4-engined, all-metal, planes had been developed as civilian airliners before the war and converted to extremely effective long-range maritime bombers. Between these three,

**The 'Scourge of the
Atlantic' – the Focke-Wulf
bf200 Kondor converted
from a civil airliner into a
deadly maritime predator.**

Germany had already sunk more than 800 ships carrying vital supplies across the North Atlantic to Britain.

So, on 9th March 1941 Bomber Command received orders, which had emanated direct from the Prime Minister, to concentrate the major part of their efforts for the next four months on destruction of these three menaces and the sites of their manufacture. The shipyards which were building the U-boats and the factories which were manufacturing their diesel engines were therefore heavily bombed as were the ports where the surface raiders might be lurking or where they might receive succour.

On 30th June 1941 Germany invaded Russia and, by the time Bomber Command's four-month campaign against the Atlantic marauders had finished in July, the bulk of Germany's might was being directed to the Eastern Front. On 9th July Bomber Command received a government directive to concentrate the major part of their effort on disrupting the enemy's transport network and to "destroying the morale of the civilian population as a whole and of the industrial workers in particular."

With better weather the bomber offensive increased as did its losses which were largely due to the growing experience and finesse of the *Luftwaffe's* nightfighters. On 1st October 1940 Helmut Lent had arrived at Deelen as *Staffelkapitan* of 6./NJG 1. He was now a fully-trained nightfighter pilot with eight kills behind him but it was to be a further seven months before he would make another. Bomber Command's activities over the winter months, largely confined to the synthetic oil installations and shipyards, were obviously less intensive but bombers were still being shot down and it must have seemed to Lent that his good fortune had changed.

From the early days of operations from Deelen the nightfighters were working in conjunction with the ground defences which would direct the pilots to a radio beacon round which they would circle until they were vectored from the ground to their target. As well as target location, the nightfighter pilots tended to rely upon ground control for navigational support; Helmut, however, placed great importance on self reliance and preferred, wherever possible, to do things himself. His reluctance to accept assistance from the ground may, possibly, have contributed to his lack of success during this period.

After the busy and successful days of daytime flying during the Norwegian Campaign, his new role as a nightfighter was proving frustrating and demoralising to the point that he put in an application to return to a daytime unit. However, this was refused and on 12th May 1941 his luck changed and he shot down two Wellingtons of No. 40 Squadron returning from a raid on Hamburg. These were his first night-time kills and dispelled whatever jinx he may have felt possessed him and removed any doubts he had about his ability as a nightfighter.

From here he never looked back; in June he had three kills including two Short Stirlings, the first to be shot down by his *staffel*. The RAF had just started introducing the new generation of heavy, four-engined bombers – the Stirling and the Handley-Page Halifax. The Avro Manchester, which was also coming into service, had only two engines which proved inadequate and it was developed into the four-engined Lancaster which proved to be the finest of them all.

Short Stirling bombers.

Both the Stirlings of No. 7 Squadron put up a good fight. The first, flown by Squadron Leader W T C Searle, with its port inner engine in flames, escaped from Lent's attention by flying into the flak barrage above Bremen where he knew his attacker would not follow him. The aircraft crash landed the other side of the city and the crew survived and became prisoners-of-war. To Helmut Lent's relief, the crew reported that they had been shot down by a Messerschmitt 110 so the victory was credited to him and not to the ground gunners! The second Stirling, flown by Flying Officer Valentine Hartwright, was not so lucky and crashed in flames killing all the crew but not before the rear gunner had disabled one of Lent's engines causing him to leave the fray and make a forced belly landing. He and his *funker* were uninjured. In a letter to his parents Helmut quixotically attributed his success to Lena, his 'little bride to be' who had visited him at the weekend. His marriage plans were now known and accepted in his family despite their rather guarded reception in the early days of their courtship.

On 1st July 1941, Helmut was appointed as *Staffelkapitan* of 4.NJG/1 at Leeuwarden which was the most distinguished squadron of the group with 27 victories already to its credit. There were several pilots in the *staffel* who had already qualified as 'aces' – *Oberfeldwebel* Paul Gildner with 13 kills; *Feldwebel* Hans Rasper with six and *Leutnant* Prince Egmont zur Lippe-Weissenfeld with seven. These, and others in the *staffel*, would accumulate huge numbers of victories in the months ahead becoming household names in Germany and national heroes though none would survive the war. Helmut with twelve victories behind him fitted very comfortably into this elite coterie.

During July Helmut, leading from the front as usual, acquired another seven kills including, on 8th, a Whitley flown by Flight Lieutenant Charles Petley, the Cambridge double first who had flown on operations with Alec during 1940. He was shot down one kilometre north-west of Orvelte in The Netherlands and is buried with three members of his crew, Sergeants Marshall, Lightley and Wilson at the nearby Westerbork General Cemetery. The wireless operator, Sergeant Reg Luce survived, though badly injured, and was sent to a POW camp after a lengthy period in hospital during which he had been operated on by a German doctor. Two nights later Helmut shot down another Wellington; it was his sixteenth, and very nearly his last, victory.

During this period Helmut was flying a Dornier 215 which carried a crew of three; in addition to Walter Kubisch, his trusty *funker*, he had a *bordmechaniker,* flight engineer, *Feldwebel* Matschuk. At 2.15 am he

Dornier 215.

AUSTRALIAN WAR MEMORIAL

intercepted a Wellington of No. 40 Squadron which was part of a force of 57 aircraft returning from a largely ineffective raid on Osnabrück. As he closed in for the kill he came under intensive and well directed fire from the Wellington's rear gunner which inflicted serious wounds on Kubisch and Matschuk though he himself miraculously escaped with several small wounds from flying splinters. Lent described this as his most dangerous encounter so far and there can be little doubt that he was lucky to escape with his life. Walter Kubisch was in hospital for a long time with head wounds which nearly cost him his sight and did not fly again with Lent for several months. The pilot of the Wellington, Flying Officer G C Conran, managed to make a crash landing; he was captured and sent to *Stalag Luft 3* in Sagan, Poland which achieved fame after the war as the site of two famous escapes which were later dramatised and made into films – *The Great Escape* and *The Wooden Horse*.

On 13th July, in spite of his injuries incurred three days earlier, Helmut was flying again and at 0055 on 13th he closed in on a Hampden of No. 59 Squadron, one of a force of 61 aircraft en route for Bremen. The pilot was Pilot Officer Edward Vivian, a 26 year-old South African from Johannesburg; the second pilot was Sergeant Kenneth Lord and there were two Wireless Operator/Air Gunners, Flight Sergeant Jack Guest from Sheffield and Sergeant H Jackson from West Hampstead.

Hadley-Page Hampden medium bombers.

RAF OFFICIAL PHOTOGRAPHER B J DAVENTRY

Sergeant Jackson's real name was Israel Jacobovitch, son of Isaac and Miriam Jacobovitch of West Hampstead but, for reasons already mentioned, he flew under a non-Jewish alias in case he should be captured by the Germans. The need for this subterfuge had not diminished: by the summer of 1941 the Nazis' persecution of the Jews had reached appalling new proportions and at the end of the month Hitler instructed SS General Reinhard Heydrich to submit plans for the 'final solution' – the complete extermination of the race. As it was, poor Sergeant Jacobovitch had no need of his alias as he, and the rest of the crew, were killed.

Next, three days later, was another Wellington, this time from No. 104 Squadron, flown by 21 year-old Pilot Officer William Rowse from Rugby. He was killed together with his second pilot, Sergeant Frederick Harmer from Kingsbury, Middlesex, his navigator, Pilot Officer John Monks from Bristol, two wireless operators/air gunners, Sergeants William Everest from Coventry and John Reynolds from Manchester and air gunner Sergeant Laurence Coogan from Birkenhead.

The eleven airmen from these two aircraft, shot down by Lent within three days of each other, lie in a communal grave in the west corner of the General Cemetery in the little town of Veendam, some 20 kilometres south-east of Groningen and 70 kilometres east of Lent's base at Leeuwarden.

On 25th July Helmut accounted for another Wellington of No. 57 Squadron and in August he had two victories – A Whitley of No. 51 Squadron on 15th and a Hampden of No. 49 Squadron on 29th. The following day he was notified that he had been awarded the Knight's Cross of the Iron Cross a high honour to which every German serviceman aspired.

The Iron Cross. After the war recipients were not allowed by law to wear their decoration because of the swastika in the centre. A politically correct version with an oak leaf cluster was substituted.

Helmut had been awarded the Iron Cross 2nd Class in September 1939 which had been 'upgraded' to 1st Class in May 1940 and this, The Knight's Cross level, was a further accolade. The citation recorded that he had destroyed a total of 21 enemy aircraft and that: "His score of thirteen enemy bombers in ten weeks is the current result of his heroic operational dedication."

The Order was worn prominently at the neck which gave rise to a great deal of chaffing within the armed services where it was referred to as the *Blechkrawatte,* tin necktie, and its holders were said to suffer from *Halsschmerzen,* throat trouble. Notwithstanding this, it was very highly coveted and worn with understandable pride.

A heavy raid on Berlin on 7th/8th September gave the nightfighters a new opportunity for successful actions. The force of 197 bombers was directed to three separate targets in Berlin and, with good visibility, results were fair within the context of the time. Hits on four munitions factories were claimed as well as several transport and public utilities. The cost to the bomber force, however, was high with 15 aircraft lost of which Lent accounted for three. The first, on 7th, was a Whitley of No. 78 Squadron and on 8th he shot down two Wellingtons within an hour of each other.

The first of these, from No.9 Squadron, Honington, was flown by 20 year-old Sergeant Jack Saich DFM from Great Easton, Essex. He had completed his mission and was returning home at an altitude of 16,000 feet when he was intercepted by Lent over the village of Drachstencompagnie about 8 miles south-east of Leeuwarden. Helmut came in from behind and below and delivered a burst of fire which killed the rear gunner, Sergeant Alan MacDonald from Ayrshire. He then came in again for a more leisurely and unopposed volley which sent the aircraft falling steeply to earth with a long smoke trail. The whole crew was killed: Sergeants William Balls from Great Yarmouth and Eric Trott from Sheffield, both Wireless Operators/Air Gunners and both aged 20; Sergeant Robert Banks, 21, from Wilmslow, the second pilot; Flight Sergeant Walter Lowe, 28, from Blackpool, the navigator, as well as Sergeants Saich and MacDonald.

They lie together, the only British occupants, in the Opsterland General Cemetery in the village of Gorredijk near to where they crashed.

Helmut's final victory in September 1941 was a Wellington from

Alec's old Squadron, No. 115, from Marham and on the following day he left Leeuwarden to start his three-week *Hochzeitsurlaub* or Wedding Leave.

If an officer wished to marry in the Third Reich it was necessary for his bride-to-be to be demonstrably Aryan with no trace of jewish blood. As Helmut's fiancée was Russian by birth she had to undergo a rigorous investigation before permission for the marriage could be granted. Documents detailing her life and background, including a Certificate of Genealogy which was a legal document confirming that she had no jewish ancestors on either her father's or her mother's sides of the family, were duly submitted and examined. Eventually it was accepted that she was of Aryan descent and permission for the marriage was received from the Commander-in-Chief's office. So on 10th September 1941 Helmut Lent and Helene Senokosnikova were married at Wellingsbüttel, a suburb of Hamburg where Lena was living at the time.

Helmut returned to Leeuwarden in time to take his share in the next major swarm of bombers on the night of 12th/13th October. A force of 373 aircraft, the largest force yet despatched by Bomber Command, set out for Germany that night in conditions of poor visibility. Of the total, 152 were sent to Nuremberg, the first major raid on that city, with smaller forces of 99 and 79 targetting Bremen and a chemical factory at Hüls respectively. None of the raids was successful but the most important one, to Nuremberg, was a classic example of how appallingly inaccurate the RAF's bombing was in the early years of the war without any sophisticated system of navigation and target location to assist the crews.

Only a few bombs actually fell on Nuremberg, killing one person and injuring six, but extensive damage was done to the small towns of Lauingen, 65 miles from the target, and Lauffen, 95 miles away. To the bewilderment of its inhabitants Launingen, which had no military or industrial installations, was attacked for four consecutive hours. Both these towns, like Nuremberg, were situated on wide rivers and it is thought that one or more hopelessly lost aircraft may have thought they had identified the target and, once they had dropped a few incendiaries, others were deceived by the fires and bombed the same positions.

On the way home the bombers then had to run the gauntlet with the nightfighters; eight aircraft of the Nuremberg force were lost and another five crashed on their return to England. At six minutes past midnight Helmut intercepted and shot down a Wellington of No. 40 Squadron and 27 minutes later a Hampden of No. 144 Squadron. Both crews were killed.

Though the crews of the British bombers and the German nightfighters were deadly enemies, intent on destroying one another, each had a great respect for the other and an understanding of the fact that they were both doing the same job albeit under different colours. The hatred felt by German civilians for the 'Terror Bombers', which sometimes put downed crews in danger of being lynched by angry civilian mobs, was not shared by the *Luftwaffe* personnel who regarded them almost as kindred spirits and sympathised to some extent with their predicament. In a letter to Nessie at the end of 1940 Alec had written:

"The crews of these night-fighters are the cream of the German Air Force. They are the thing we fear the most. Though we think of nothing other than killing them, and them us, I expect they are decent fellows just like our own with much the same habits and aspirations. It is sad that we have to fight good people so like ourselves."

Handley-Page Halifax.

RAF OFFICIAL PHOTOGRAPHER

In the early hours of 13th October a member of Helmut's *staffel, Leutnant* Leopold Fellerer, shot down a Halifax of No. 76 Squadron based at Middleton St. George. The Canadian pilot, Flight Sergeant Elmer Muttart RCAF, was killed in trying to save his crew in a crash landing on the Dutch coast south-west of Leeuwarden but the other seven members of the crew got out of the crash and were captured. The rear gunner, Sergeant John Duffield, sustained some injuries and was taken into the sickbay at Leeuwarden.

The rest of the crew were entertained royally for the evening in the *Luftwaffe* Officers' Mess at Leuwarden. In a letter to his parents Helmut told of the good evening they had enjoyed and mentioned that some of the English prisoners had made a very good impression. In an almost word-for-word repetition of Alec's sentiments he added:

"It really is a cause for regret that we have to fight against such men."

The following day he visited Sergeant Duffield in the sickbay and introduced himself and then visited him every day until he was transferred some six days later. Duffield later related how Lent asked him if there was anything he could do for him. The room was very hot and stuffy as the window had been sealed and Duffield asked if it might be opened for some fresh air. Lent laughed and told him that the medical staff were afraid he might escape. Nevertheless, he arranged for the window to be opened.

During his time in command of 4./NJG 1 Helmut had come to the attention of higher authorities both as a very successful nightfighter pilot and as an excellent leader of men who was liked and respected by all the officers and men of his *staffel*. With glowing references from his superiors, and at the unusually young age of 23, he was appointed as *Gruppen-komandeur* of II./NJG 2 in the rank of *Hauptmann*. A *Gruppe* consisted of three *staffeln*, each nominally of twelve aircraft, making a total force of about 36 aircraft together with their air and ground crews and supporting services personnel *(see diagram on page 251)*.

When Helmut took over his new appointment on 1st November 1941 he had a total of 26 kills. His new position necessarily meant that he would have to devote more of his time to command and less to operational flying but on 8th he notched up his final victory of the year with a Wellington of No. 75 (New Zealand) Squadron flown by Flight Sergeant John Black RNZAF. It was on its way to Berlin as part of a huge force of 392 aircraft, yet another record, and the results of the raid were to be as deplorable as those of the Nuremberg raid in the previous month.

Of the 392 aircraft, 223 were split between raids on Cologne and Mannheim and 169 were sent to Berlin. Visibility was dreadful and only 73 of these managed to reach the target area. Their bombs were scattered across the city with very little effect for the force employed. Only eleven German civilians were killed in Berlin whereas about 60 British airmen were lost in the 21 aircraft destroyed by flak and nightfighters.

Of the entire force, including the Cologne and Mannheim contingents, a total of 37 aircraft were lost. There had been considerable dissension among the group commanders about the wisdom of mounting

**Air Marshal Sir Richard Peirse KCB, DSO, AFC,
Commander-in-Chief Bomber Command 1940-1942.**

RAF OFFICIAL PHOTOGRAPHER

any raids at all that night in view of the adverse weather conditions and it is probable that several of the aircraft which failed to return had ditched in the North Sea due to icing or having run out of fuel.

It was a bad night for the RAF but if was a good night for the *Luftwaffe*. Helmut Lent's *staffel* accounted for a total of nine aircraft including his own Wellington and a Stirling shot down by *Leutnant* Fellerer after a series of five or six attacks on it. Among his comrades Fellerer was lightheartedly becoming known as the *Viermot* specialist meaning an expert in destroying the big four-engined bombers which were appearing in increasing numbers over Germany.

The losses of aircraft in the Berlin raid represented 12.4% of the force engaged, more than double the greatest loss in any previous operation. The following day the C-in-C Bomber Command, Air Marshal Sir Richard Peirse, was summoned to Chequers by the Prime Minister to answer some difficult questions. Results of bombing raids had become unacceptably low and casualties unacceptably high and, clearly, something had to be done about it.

Chapter 8 – Area Bombing

David Bensusan-Butt was a civil servant in the War Cabinet Secretariat acting as private secretary to Lord Cherwell, the government's leading scientific adviser and a close friend of Winston Churchill. In July 1941 Cherwell commissioned Bensusan-Butt to undertake an in-depth study of the effectiveness of Bomber Command's operations and an examination of how actual results compared with the claims of the aircrews.

To do this he analysed the damage recorded in over 4,000 photographs taken during 100 bombing sorties during June and July and compared it with the aircrews' post-operational reports. His findings, published on 18th August 1941 as *The Butt Report*, were disheartening though they only confirmed what the aircrews had known themselves for some time. Claims of successes by aircrews had always been optimistic – the kills recorded by the Battle of Britain pilots had been wildly exaggerated – and the report concluded that only about one third of aircraft claiming to have reached their target had actually got within five miles of it. Further statistics showed that even worse results could be expected in poor weather conditions or where identification of the target was difficult; hence, results for raids on the Channel Ports – close to home and with easily recognised coastline features – were not too bad with two out of three bombers reaching their target. On the other hand raids on the Rhur, with its homogeneous acres of industrial activity with few landmarks to assist with target location, showed that only one in ten aircraft hit the mark.

Butt's conclusions sent shockwaves through the government and were, naturally, hotly disputed by the RAF command which commissioned its own report. This, though failing to address past failures, outlined plans for the future from which it was predicted that, with a force of 4,000 aircraft, Bomber Command could win the war in six months. There then ensued an acrimonious battle between those who felt that the funding received by Bomber Command could be more effectively used in other branches of the Services, and the RAF commanders who fought fiercely to retain their share of the cake. A principal advocate of the former view was Sir Henry Tizard

Professor F A Lindemann, later Lord Cherwell *(extreme left)* **with the Prime Minister and senior service officers at an anti-aircraft demonstration June 1941**

who urged the cabinet to reduce the scale of the bombing offensive. To counter these arguments and set minds at rest regarding Butt's conclusions, Lord Cherwell, in March 1942, presented his own proposals to Churchill in what later became known as *The Dehousing Paper*. This advocated no reduction in Bomber Command's funding and that its aim should now be the destruction of housing in Germany's major cities which Cherwell saw as the quickest way to destroy the enemy's morale and thereby win the war.

Frederick Lindemann, Lord Cherwell, had been born in Germany and educated at the University of Berlin but had a deep hatred of the Nazi regime. However, he was arrogant and elitist and regarded working class people, blacks and homosexuals with complete contempt. Despite his loathing of the Nazis, he seemed to share Hitler's philosophy on the improvement of the race by selective breeding. It was therefore no surprise that he advocated that bombing should be directed at working class areas where housing was packed more tightly together and the maximum destruction could be achieved.

RAF OFFICIAL PHOTOGRAPHER

**Air Chief Marshal Sir Arthur Harris,
Commander-in-Chief Bomber Command 1942-1945**

The two opposing views were so passionately held that a High Court Judge, Mr Justice Singleton, was appointed to examine the arguments and reached the conclusion that if Russia could continue to keep its German invaders occupied on land:

> **". . . I doubt whether Germany will stand 12 or 18 months' continuous, intensified and increased bombing, affecting, as it must, her war production, her power of resistance, her industries and her will to resist (by which I mean morale)."**

Cherwell's proposals were therefore accepted and Area Bombing of residential districts became official policy.

On 8th January 1942, with the horror of the November Berlin raid still fresh in mind, Sir Richard Peirse was removed from his position as Commander-in-Chief Bomber Command and, after a short interregnum, was replaced on 22nd February by Air Chief Marshal Sir Arthur Harris. Recorded in history as 'Bomber Harris' but known universally in the service as 'The Chief' or more malevolently 'The Butcher', Harris was to become a dedicated exponent of area bombing though he had played no part in its initial sanction and introduction.

Harris was uncompromising about the aims of his new command – to destroy residential areas in enemy cities, to kill civilians, to create a hitherto unprecedented refugee crisis for the enemy, all designed to destroy their morale. These aims were not to be regarded as a spin-off from attacks on military or industrial targets, they were the aim in themselves. He recorded his justification and announced his intentions in his famous statement when he took command:

"The Nazis entered this war under the rather childish delusion that they were going to bomb everyone else, and nobody was going to bomb them. At Rotterdam, London, Warsaw and half a hundred other places, they put their rather naive theory into operation. They sowed the wind, and now they are going to reap the whirlwind."

With his very long experience of bombing technique, Harris soon implemented major changes in Bomber Command's *modus operandi*. Concentration was the keyword of his strategy: the former practice of small bomber forces each being sent to a different target was abandoned and the total force of available aircraft was sent to a single target to deliver its loads over a much shorter period of time than previously. This introduced a greater risk of mid-air collision which Harris considered a justifiable risk for the advantages gained.

Now that the directed aims of Bomber Command had been clearly stated, Harris also set about refining bombing technique to cause maximum damage in residential areas. Uncontrolled fire was now seen as the most effective way of causing devastation so the quantity of incendiaries used

Assembly of Wellington bombers.

RAF OFFICIAL PHOTOGRAPHER

by aircraft was increased. The practice of using high explosive bombs to blow off the roofs of houses to open them up for the incendiaries was already well established. Harris refined this principle and recognised that the initial high explosive bombardment would also crater the streets and block them with fallen masonry which would impede the movement of fire appliances. This gave the fires a chance to get established and to reach the intensity where they would create a wind force around them which would be drawn in and fan the flames further to develop eventually into the much-feared firestorms.

When Harris took over, the total bomber force available for night operations was less than 500. Though production had been going flat out, this number had not increased during 1941 due to the heavy losses and the necessary transfer of aircraft to Coastal Command to combat the U-boat menace. However the heavy, four-engined bombers were now coming off the production lines and, as these had a greater bomb carrying capacity, the RAF was able to deliver an ever increasing tonnage of bombs.

Also arriving at about the same time as its new C-in-C, the first production models of the 'Gee' system were being received by Bomber Command and installed in operational squadrons. 'Gee' had been under development for some time and consisted of a radio set which would receive synchronised pulses transmitted by a chain of transmitters on the ground in widely spaced parts of the country. These signals enabled the navigator to fix the position of his aircraft with a greater degree of accuracy than had ever previously been possible. The effectiveness of the system decreased with distance from the transmitter chain but with a range of about 300 miles it still provided a major breakthrough in target location and brought many bombers safely home in poor conditions.

When Alec rejoined No. 115 Squadron in April 1942 the squadron was equipped with the Wellington Mark III which had replaced the Mark 1C in which he had flown in 1940. The Mk.III was fitted with more powerful Bristol engines – the Hercules III of 1,425 hp instead of the Pegasus XVIII of 1,050 hp. The service ceiling had been increased from 18,000 ft. to 22,700 ft. and the maximum speed from 254 mph to 261 mph. The Mk.III had extra armour plating, balloon cable cutters and windscreen wipers but, from Alec's point of view, the most important improvement was the fitting of the Fraser-Nash FN20A rear turret with four machine guns in place of the 2-gun FN5 on the Mk. 1C. Although still no match for the *Luftwaffe's* larger bore guns, the new turret doubled the firepower available to the rear gunner. So in this much improved aircraft he commenced his second operational tour on 29th April 1942.

Alec was delighted to find that his flight commander in 'A' Flight was Squadron Leader Alan Cousens with whom he had flown on the Queen Wilhelmina's birthday flight over Holland in the previous year. Cousens was similarly pleased to see Alec joining his flight and immediately assigned him as rear gunner in his own crew which he was forming up.

**A Fraser-Nash FN20 4-gun tail turret preserved at the
Imperial War Museum, Duxford.**

ALAN WILSON, HAWKEYE UK

Squadron Leader (later Wing Commander) Alan George Seymour Cousens DSO, DFC, RAF

MICHAEL COUSENS

Alan Cousens was a regular airman who had enlisted in 1930 at the age of seventeen and had served in the ranks for ten years in Britain and the Far East before being commissioned in 1940. He had joined 115 Squadron from Headquarters No. 3 Group, where he had been Group Navigation Officer, only three weeks before Alec's arrival. Though he had been an acting squadron leader for some time, his substantive rank was still flight lieutenant.

Alan was the third son of Lieutenant Colonel Gordon Bryce Cousens who had won a Military Cross in the First World War after which he obtained a government appointment in the Far East. His two elder sons were placed in boarding school in England and Alan, who was only six, accompanied his parents to China. In 1939 when he was an acting sergeant in No. 38 Squadron at Marham, Alan married Nan Phyllis Ferbes at Bristol who in due course presented him with a son, Michael.

With 38 Squadron at Marham, in the ten months from August 1940 to June 1941, Alan acquired a reputation as a meticulous navigator and inspirational leader. His long service in peacetime as well as war placed him in a position of influence and respect among officers and men alike most of whom were in the air force for 'hostilities only'.

On his first day back at Marham, before he had even had time to unpack his kit, Alec was bundled into the rear turret of Alan Cousens's Wellington X3644 and was on his way to bomb the Gnome-Rhone factory in Paris. This company manufactured radial aircraft engines which were in use throughout the world and which the Germans had started to use in some of their own aircraft; they had also forced the factory to start building the BMW 801 engine and, although the workers conspired to slow down production as much as they could get away with, the factory was still making a considerable contribution to the German war effort.

For the next week Alan Cousens took his crew out on working-up flights so they could brush up on their flying and bombing and get used to each other's ways. Though a navigator himself, the squadron leader was, unusually, captain of the aircraft and carried another navigator to free him for the requirements of command. There was therefore only one pilot who was officially designated as 'second pilot'; this was 22 year-old Pilot Officer John Frederick Stock RAFVR who, like Alec, had enlisted at the beginning of the war and been commissioned from the ranks; he had been educated at Haileybury. In 1939, with war imminent, his family had returned from Kenya where they had been coffee planters and had bought the Wellington Hotel in Boscastle, a picture-postcard village on the north coast of Cornwall.

In the last war, Johnny's father, Frederick, had been a victim of German bombing: while stationed at RAF Ford in West Sussex, the aerodrome had been attacked by a Zeppelin and Frederick had taken cover in a shelter with six NCOs. A bomb had dropped near the shelter the blast from which shattered his lower jaw and killed five of the six airmen beside him. Frederick had a score to settle with the Germans and must have felt some satisfaction when his son became a bomber pilot.

**Pilot Officer John Frederick Stock
RAFVR**

ROD AND ANNE KNIGHT, BOSCASTLE

**John Stock climbing over the bulwark of a French fishing boat
having been rescued from his ditched aircraft during a training flight.**

Johnny had done his flying training at No. 14 Service Flying Training School at Cranfield in Bedfordshire and at No.20 Operational Training Unit. During the course of his training he had had to make a forced landing in the North Sea which had been good experience for what was to come later. He and the rest of the crew were picked up by a French fishing boat.

At some point in his career, possibly at Cranfield, Johnny had met Guy Gibson, of later Dambusters fame, who accompanied him on one leave to the Wellington Hotel in Boscastle. Gibson's entry in the visitors' book is preserved with pride to this day.

Having gained his 'Wings', Johnny was posted to No. 115 Squadron at Marham on 27th September 1941. His first operational flight was two days later when he flew as second pilot to Flight Lieutenant Foster on a bombing raid to Stettin. During October he had a further four operations as second pilot to Warrant Officer Snowden, Flight Sergeant Edwards and Sergeant Runagall in raids on St. Nazaire, Darnstadt and Duisberg.

Then on 15th November he was given his first command and took off from Marham in Wellington HZ8848 for a raid on Kiel. There were eight aircraft from 115 Squadron, five from A Flight and three from B Flight, which took off between 2130 and 2151. It was to be a long night; heavy cloud over the target area made accurate location impossible and much time was expended in circling round trying to find a break in the cloud. Three aircraft gave up and diverted to secondary targets. By the time the returning force reached the English coast they were dangerously short of fuel. Six of the eight made it home landing between 0524 and 0720 after having been in the air for between eight to ten hours. Sergeant John Horsley, a 21 year-old pilot from Derbyshire failed to return; he and his crew were never found and were assumed to have ditched in the North Sea. Johnny Stock was more fortunate; he had almost reached the English coast when his engines died.

Remembering his previous experience and the instructions he had received during training, he glided down to a forced landing, parallel to the line of the waves, in the sea just off Whitby in North Yorkshire. A landing at right angles to the waves, he knew, could result in the aircraft hitting a crest, breaking in half and sinking immediately. Assisted by his second pilot, Sergeant Weller, he made a successful belly landing and the aircraft stayed afloat long enough for the whole crew to evacuate into their inflatable dinghy.

They were later picked up by a Norwegian destroyer. Johnny had managed to save his crew with a textbook ditching but it was, nevertheless, a rather ignominious end to his first operation as captain.

During December he made a further four operational flights to Wilhelmshaven and the French Biscay Ports. On the second of these he had to abandon the operation due to an internal failure and returned to Marham with his bombs. He had therefore undertaken twelve sorties in his first operational tour by the end of the year when he was transferred to the station administrative staff where he remained for four months until Alan Cousens selected him as the pilot of his crew and got him back into the air on 29th April.

Apart from two bombing raids during May, the whole month was spent in intensive training. Usually Squadron Leader Cousens was in command but for some of the flights he stood down and let Pilot Officer Stock take over. Bombing and air firing practice were undertaken again and again; on one occasion they practised formation flying and on another fighter tactics with a Spitfire playing the part of a German nightfighter.

Alec.

During these training flights the squadron leader was constantly assessing his crew members with the object of finalising on a really good regular team. Various navigators and front gunners flew in his crew during this period but Pilot Officer George Whittaker soon proved himself as a man who could work in perfect harmony with the rest of the team and was established as their regular Wireless Operator/Gunner. George was 25 years old and was a Lancastrian from Accrington. He had enlisted in 1938 and during his first operational tour with No. 37 Squadron had been awarded the Distinguished Flying Medal. Like Alec, he had spent a year between tours as an instructor and had been commissioned in March.

The first of the two May operations in which Alec took part was a raid on Stuttgart. Between 2130 and 2220 on the evening of 6th May fourteen aircraft from 115 Squadron took off joining up with a total force of 97 bombers from other stations. The operation was to be a classic example of the difficulties of accurate target location and of the effectiveness of Germany's deception measures.

In the summer of 1940 *Luftwaffe* General Hugo Sperrie had ordered the construction of dummy target sites for all major industrial targets within his command area. The initiative soon spread to other vulnerable areas throughout Germany. The sites were extremely elaborate reconstructions of actual targets nearby with the object of luring RAF bombers away from the real target. The construction teams went to great lengths to make the dummies as realistic as possible: replica factory buildings and railway stations were linked by dummy tramlines and electrical circuits created sparks to simulate the sparks omitted from the overhead power lines used by the trams. The phony towns were surrounded by anti-aircraft batteries, as a real target would be, and the area was very dimly lit to simulate a poorly-observed blackout.

Within a year these dummy targets were diverting a large volume of the RAF's bomb loads from genuine targets throughout Germany; there were eleven such sites around Hamburg alone. As some of the bomber crews started to get wise to them, the dummies were augmented with fire pits – huge stone enclosures which would be filled with combustible material and set alight as the bombers approached. In poor visibility it was all too easy to assume that these great conflagrations had been started by the bombers ahead which had identified the target. Successive waves of aircraft would bomb the same position thereby increasing the intensity of the blaze and attracting more aircraft from further away.

In the *Luftwaffe* area which included Stuttgart there were nine dummy targets each of which had the codename of a South American country. The Messerschmitt factory at Augsburg had a replica called 'Argentina' and a complete dummy airfield near Schwabisch Hall was called 'Costa Rica'. The dummy for Stuttgart was an elaborate reconstruction of the city's main railway station at a town called Lauffen some twenty miles north of Stuttgart which was supported by a large firepit nearby. The site was codenamed 'Brasilien'.

Stuttgart was a notoriously difficult city to locate even in good visibility and on the night of 6th/7th May a thick ground haze over the target area made positive identification impossible. On their return, Squadron Leader Cousens, in common with most of the other captains, could only report that they had "dropped their bombs on visual observation and observed bursts in a built-up area". None of the crews could report a positive identification of the target or observation of any significant damage. German records examined after the war showed that not a single bomb from the raid had actually fallen on Stuttgart. However, Heilbronn, a city some five miles north of 'Brasilien', sustained heavy and prolonged attacks during the night and, on this occasion, the RAF bombers had clearly been fooled by the Lauffen decoy. This was not the only instance: after the war it was also revealed that the town of Lauffen had been bombed 37 times instead of Stuttgart.

One aircraft from 115 Squadron, Pilot Officer George, had to turn back and jettison their bombs due to engine trouble. Two aircraft failed to return: Flight Lieutenant John Sword, a 23 year-old Cambridge Graduate from Chipping Norton, was lost with all his crew as was 25 year-old New Zealander, Flight Lieutenant Nathaniel Paterson.

This raid on Stuttgart was the third of three undertaken during May all of which had been equally ineffective. The Bosch electrical factory, which was the most important target in the city for the raiders, was completely untouched but on all three occasions the Lauffen decoy took a serious hammering. Then on 19th May a force of 197 aircraft, including 12

A Wellington of Central Gunnery School.

from 115 Squadron, were sent on a raid to Mannheim. Squadron Leader Cousens and his crew were not on operations that night. The weather was much the same as it had been for the Stuttgart raid with very bad visibility over the target. Three quarters of the aircraft engaged claimed on their return to have hit the target but when the film from their cameras had been developed the shots showed blazing forest areas rather than built-up city centres.

Air Marshal Harris was furious; May had been an almost completely impotent month for Bomber Command with the enemy's decoy subterfuge winning at every round and the loss of over 40 RAF aircraft. Somewhat unfairly he blamed the crews:

> **"It is apparent from the night photographs and from the reports of crews, that almost the whole effort was wasted in bombing large fires in the local forests. and possibly decoy fires. Nevertheless, in spite of the now incontrovertible evidence that this is what in fact occurred, the reports of the crews on their return from the raid were most definite in very many cases that they had reached the town and bombed it.... The cause of this failure is beyond doubt to be found in the easy manner in which crews are misled by decoy fires or by fires in the wrong place ... somehow or other we must cure this disease, for it is a disease, of wasting bombs wholesale on decoy fires."**

Even the most experienced crews had been fooled at one time or another by German decoys and fire pits although, as the war progressed, they were becoming increasingly more adept in recognising the tell-tale signs. Just as the bomber crews were inclined to exaggerate their successes, so were the *Luftwaffe* prone to overstating the efficacy of their decoy programme. The previous summer *Reich Minister* Joseph Goebbels had recorded:

> **"We cannot deny the pompous declarations of success by the RAF, because they mostly concern dummy instal-lations. The statistics mentioned by the English are totally grotesque. But perhaps they even believe them themselves."**

The bomber crews had gone as far as their eyesight, instinct and experience could take them. Now they needed radio assistance in navigation and target location. It was coming: the early versions of 'Gee' were already being installed in operational squadrons, though its range was limited, and some of the best brains in the country were working upon its refinement and development. It was only a matter of time before crews would receive the support they so desperately needed.

Chapter 9 – The First 1,000 Bomber Raid

Alec considered himself fortunate to be flying with such a reliable and experienced crew led by a captain who was held in great esteem by all who had served with him. Alec wrote to Nessie:

"The Squadron Leader is an inspirational commander. Everything he does is done to perfection and he expects the same from his crew. All the boys think the world of him and work very hard to try and achieve the standards he sets."

The regard was mutual: on 25th May Alan Cousens called Alec to his office and told him that he was going to appoint him as Gunnery Leader. This would give him responsibility for the deployment, training and discipline of all the air gunners in the squadron. His flying would be somewhat curtailed but he would fly regularly in Squadron Leader Cousens's crew and would always accompany the Wing Commander when he flew on operations, which was not very often.

Alec replied that he would really much prefer to stay where he was, in a crack and experienced crew and in a job where he felt he could make the best contribution to the squadron, and to the war.

Cousens told him that he could not refuse the appointment; it was a great honour to be offered the job of Gunnery Leader in a squadron like 115, particularly as he had been back with the squadron for such a short time and had only recently been commissioned as a Pilot Officer. His new rank would almost certainly be Flight Lieutenant, jumping Flying Officer all together, which would mean that he had been promoted from Flight Sergeant to Flight Lieutenant in less than two months – unusually swift advancement. His new pay would be 21 shillings a day, almost double what he had been paid as a Flight Sergeant.

Alec was still reluctant to abandon his gun turret but the Squadron Leader was insistent: he told him that he was the best gunner he had ever flown with, and it was his duty to pass his skills on to others. The following day he was advised by the Adjutant that his appointment as Gunnery Leader had been confirmed to start from 27th May.

The first operation in which Alec took part as Gunnery Leader, and the last in May 1942, was the most notable in Bomber Command's history to date and one which marked the start of a new strategy, a new level of success and a new confidence in the bombing offensive in the eyes of the War Cabinet and the other armed services.

Sir Arthur Harris had been conscious for some time of the need for a major demonstrable success to secure Bomber Command's place in the pecking order for funding and to quell the voices of the critics who believed that the money spent on bombers and bombing could be better spent elsewhere. This was to be the first, and most important, of his famous Thousand Bomber Raids.

Harris believed in vast numbers and although he had only 400 aircraft on his operational bombing strength, he was determined to scrape together, from all available sources, enough to make up the magical 1,000. This number, he knew, would not only do the job of massive destruction on the scale which he envisaged, but would provide a great opportunity for the publicity that the Command needed.

With 250 aircraft offered by Coastal Command and another 350 borrowed from the Operational Training Units and Conversion Units he could comfortably make up the 1,000. As far as the training units were involved, it was only necessary to take very advanced trainees who were nearing completion of their course, and what better for them than a live operation to end up with.

However, the Royal Navy still had a very proprietorial attitude towards any form of maritime aviation and were unwilling to see the war against the U-boats interrupted by the loss, albeit temporary, of 250 aircraft from Coastal Command.

Nor was the navy enthusiastic about a project which would give the RAF a great publicity boost and could result in a strengthening of their case for an increased share of the budget. They therefore refused to sanction Coastal Command's contribution.

This was a major blow to the initiative and Harris had to scrape up every aircraft he could lay his hands on. This included every serviceable plane from the training units, which would be flown on the night by crews in the very early stages of their training, and by pilots who had only recently started conversion training from twin-engined to four-engined bombers. Crews who had just completed their 30-operations tour, and had been posted for a very well-earned rest as instructors, found themselves back on operations. By every means possible, Harris eventually managed to put together a force of 1,047 bombers. The raid had originally been intended for Hamburg but when weather conditions necessitated a change to Cologne it was something of a relief to the crews as Cologne was within 'Gee's' range. Most of the operational squadrons involved were now equipped with 'Gee' which meant that the experienced crews who led the attack would be certain to locate and identify the targets correctly.

Harris's new strategy included the formation of the 'Bomber Stream'. This meant that the entire force would attack in a concentrated phalanx with every aircraft having its own time slot and height to minimise the risk of mid-air collisions. In the past a large raid would take several hours for the whole force to pass over the target; Harris expected this to be reduced to a maximum of 90 minutes. The reasons for this huge concentration of fast moving attackers were twofold: firstly the chain of German nightfighter stations which stretched along the Dutch coast were divided into several control boxes or zones *(see diagram on page 250)*. Each box had a ground control unit which would direct the nightfighters on to the bombers and was capable of undertaking six such directions in one hour. With the entire force crossing the coast within two hours and with the stream so concentrated that it passed through a single control box, the opportunities for the nightfighters would be greatly reduced. The diagrams on the following two pages show the breakdown of the force and will give some impression of its immense size.

The second advantage of Harris's Bomber Stream was that the sheer volume of aircraft and the speed at which the force would pass over the target area would overwhelm the anti-aircraft batteries, and greatly reduce their operational window, just as the massive damage the force would inflict on the ground would overwhelm the fire and emergency services. The Bomber Stream therefore promised fewer losses and greater damage to the enemy.

THE FIRST 1,000 BOMBER RAID, 3Oth MAY 1942

602 WELLINGTONS

79 HAMPDENS

28 WHITLEYS

46 MANCHESTERS

73 LANCASTERS

88 STIRLINGS

131 HALIFAXES

709 MEDIUM AND 338 HEAVY BOMBERS – TOTAL 1,047

As instructed in the Form B826 received from Headquarters 3 Group, the squadrons at Marham scraped together every single aircraft which could fly and manned them with whoever they could lay their hands on. No. 115 Squadron mustered 18 aircraft, 10 from 'A' Flight and 8 from 'B'. Fitters had to rush to complete maintenance work on aircraft which were not due out until the next night and men about to go on leave had their departure postponed. Seven of the eighteen crews detailed had flown on operations the previous night and would normally have been stood down.

Alec's plane, crewed in the main by experienced, second-tour men, was to be one of the leaders and was the fifth aircraft to take off at 2300. The whole squadron was airborne within one hour and twenty minutes. Squadron Leader Cousens had his three 'regulars' with him – Pilot Officers Stock, Whittaker and Ollar and there were two 'strangers' in the crew – Flying Officer Nicholson as navigator and Sergeant Margerison in the front turret.

The weather was fair and 'Gee' enabled the leaders to locate and positively identify the targets. Three quarters of their bomb loads were incendiaries which soon created bright fires below so the following, and less experienced, crews had no difficulty in knowing where to drop their loads. The first wave of bombers arrived over Cologne at 0047 on the 31st and the entire stream had passed through within the 90 minutes specified by the Commander-in-Chief. The force dropped 1,455 tons of bombs including 970 tons of incendiaries and the scale of destruction was prodigious: 2,500 fires were started; 12,840 buildings were destroyed including 2,500 industrial and commercial premises; 38,000 civilian homes were hit 13,000 of which were completely destroyed; 45,000 people were bombed out, 500 killed and 5,000 injured. Whole areas of the city were reduced to rubble, impeding the overstretched emergency services and causing an enormous flow of refugees. It was estimated that between 135,000 and 150,000 from a total population of 700,000 fled the city after the raid.

British losses were the highest ever recorded for a single operation although less than predicted. Churchill had reckoned that 100 losses would be 'acceptable'; the actual figure was 44 compared with the previous highest loss of 37 on 7th/8th November 1941. Some 22 aircraft were lost over the

Armourers loading a 250 lb. GP bomb into the bomb bay of a Wellington.

target area with the rest falling victim to flak and nightfighters on the outward and return journeys. Surprisingly, only two aircraft were lost in a collision – an impressive tribute to the careful planning of heights and time slots within the stream and the vigilance of the crews. Only one aircraft from 115 Squadron, flown by Sergeant Edwards and his crew of Sergeants Crampton, Boyle, McLeod and Sproston, failed to return.

Alec wrote to Nessie:

"You will have read in the papers about the big raid on Cologne at the weekend. It was an amazing turnout of over a thousand bombers from stations all over England. There was a full moon and we had a better view of the city than we have ever had before so there was no difficulty in finding the target – not that we would have done anyway with the skipper we have. S/L Cousens never drops his bombs in the wrong place."

The next day another 'first' was achieved by Bomber Command: five Mosquitos from No. 105 Squadron were despatched to Cologne to photograph the damage done in the big raid. This was the first operation using Mosquitos, the RAF's new superfast multi-role aircraft which was to play an important part in the air war from now on. With two powerful engines and a wooden airframe, the de Havilland Mosquito had originally been conceived as a fast precision bomber but with its speed and manoeuvrability it was soon recognised as one of the most versatile aircraft of the war which could be used as a bomber, a fighter, a pathfinder or, as in this case, for high-speed photo-reconnaissance. On this, its first operation, one of the five Mosquitos, flown by Pilot Officers Kennard and Johnson, was hit by flak and crashed into the North Sea but the other four had collected the evidence which Harris needed.

When this had been analysed, the first 1,000 Bomber Raid had to be acknowledged, even by Bomber Command's fiercest critics, to have been a great success and the future of the area bombing offensive was secured.

The second 1,000 raid was launched on 1st June just two days after the first and the results were a bitter disappointment. In spite of 'Gee' and in spite of the raid again being led by the experienced crews of No. 3 Group, a thick haze hung over the target area and none of the aircraft was able to make a positive identification. This time the force fell just short of the 1,000 with a total of 956 aircraft; 115 Squadron again contributed 18 – 10 from 'A' Flight and 8 from 'B'. Alec's aircraft X3471 took off at 2255 with a reduced crew of five – the usual team of Cousens, Stock, Whittaker and Ollar with Sergeant Slatter as navigator. None of the captains, not even Alan Cousens, could be certain they had identified the target, Essen. They bombed from 16,500 feet and on their return at 0300 could only claim that they had hit 'a built up area' and had not been able to observe any results.

Postwar analysis showed that only very minor damage had been inflicted upon Essen but several other nearby towns in the Ruhr, including Mülheim, Oberhausen, Duisburg and Gelsenkirchen, were heavily raided and had obviously been mistaken for the target by the leaders with the rest following their example. It is fortunate that this was not the first of the 1,000 raids or the future of Bomber Command's activities might have been very different. A total of 31 bombers were lost including one Wellington of 115

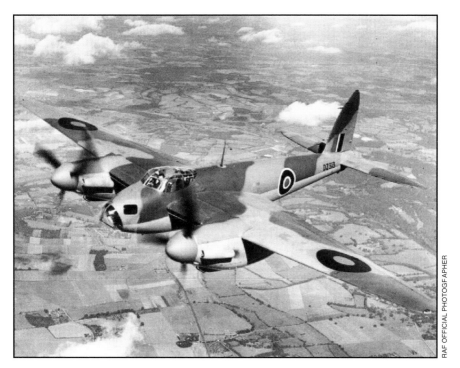

RAF OFFICIAL PHOTOGRAPHER

De Havilland Mosquito. Its high speed and manoeuvrability enabled it to be used in several different roles.

Squadron flown by Flying Officer Lyn Williams from Westfield in Surrey with his crew of Pilot Officer King, a New Zealander, and Sergeants McKellar, Strain and Kepple. With the necessity of scraping together every available aircraft for these maximum effort raids, most of the aircraft from 115 Squadron were flying five-up without a second pilot.

Alec was settling in well in his new appointment as Gunnery Leader. His operational flying was, of course, reduced which he regretted but must have been a great relief to Nessie. He only went on one more operation in June, on the 22nd to Emden as part of a force of 227 aircraft 14 of which were from 115 Squadron. Alan Cousens's plane identified the target and bombed the south-west corner of the town from 14,000 feet; it was his regular crew with Flying Officer Nicholson as navigator. On the outward journey WX3555 flown by Pilot Officer Freegard developed engine trouble and had to ditch in the sea about 60 miles north-east of Cromer. Nobody was injured and the crew was picked up by a launch of the Air Sea Rescue Service. On 24th June Alec wrote to Nessie:

"It is good to be doing the occasional operation to keep my hand in although my ground job is very satisfying too. I hope I will be able to make a contribution towards improving the squadron's efficiency still further and it is nice to feel that I am of some use to the young gunners who are new to operations and need a guiding hand to help them settle into this very lonely job."

On Friday 10th July Alec got a rare long weekend pass leaving Marham on Friday morning and returning Sunday night in time for operations the next day. It was too short to go home to Edinburgh so he spent it with his sister, Mary, in Farnborough. His brother-in-law was serving in North Africa and Mary was living with her two children and their Irish nanny in an army hiring close to the Farnborough airfield. This was naturally a target for the *Luftwaffe* and much damage had been sustained by houses in the neighbourhood though Mary's house had escaped so far. Alec also took this opportunity to leave his motorcycle under cover in Mary's garage; he did not anticipate being able to use it much during this tour and did not wish it to deteriorate still further parked in the open.

The children were delighted to see their favourite uncle and made constant demands upon his attention during his two-day stay much of which was spent on his knees 'boxing' with his five year-old nephew whom he cautioned, before he left, against riding his motorbike round the town as soon as his back was turned!

A group of 115 Squadron aircrew in 1942. Alec is second from right in the front row.

Messerschmitt bf110 of Zerstörergeschwader 1

Helmut Lent, like Alec, was also having to balance his time between operational sorties and his ground responsibilities as *Gruppenkommandeur* of 11./NJG 2. On the night of the first great 1,000 Bomber Raid he was airborne with his *staffel* from their base at Leeuwarden waiting to intercept the raiders heading for Cologne. They were to be disappointed: flying in Harris's new tight formation, the bomber stream travelled in a fairly straight line from East Anglia to Cologne crossing the Dutch coast in the region of Flushing, far to the south of Lent's patrol area. It took the same line on its return, separated by a few miles from its outward route to avoid collisions.

In the first five months of the year 1942 Helmut had personally accounted for eleven British bombers – two Whitleys, four Hampdens, two Manchesters and three Wellingtons, one of which was from No. 311 (Czech) Squadron flown by Flight Sergeant Josef Kalensky. At this stage Lent had accounted for a total of 38.

Adolf Hitler decorates three of his ace pilots at The 'Wolf's Lair' , his headquarters bunker in East Prussia.
From left: **Helmut Lent, Heinrich Setz and Friedrich Geisshardt**

June was, for a number of reasons, to be the most consequential month of his life so far. On 3rd he shot down a Hampden, one of 14 bombers destroyed in a raid on Essen and, on the following day, a Halifax of No. 76 Squadron on its way home from Bremen. Saturday 6th June was to be a true red letter day: taking off from his base at Leeuwarden just after midnight he shot down two Wellingtons heading for Essen and landed back at Leeuwarden less than two hours later before 0200. Later in the day he learnt that his wife Lena had given birth to a baby daughter whom they called Christina and, on the same momentous day, the *Führer* awarded him with the *Eichenlaub* – the Oak Leaf enhancement to his Iron Cross. He was the first nightfighter pilot to be given this honour which only 97 people had ever received.

On the following day he travelled to Hamburg to see his daughter and to spend a couple of days with Lena. From then until the end of the month he shot down a further five bombers making a total of nine in June and bringing his grand total score up to 47.

Sefton Delmer, head of he Black Propaganda department of the Political Warfare Executive.

As the climax of his *mensis mirabilis*, Helmut travelled to Rastenburg in East Prussia where a vast fortified bunker known as the *Wolfsschanze* (Wolf's Lair) had been constructed as the *Führer's* Eastern Front Headquarters. Here he was invested personally by Adolf Hitler with his *Eichenlaub* after which he was invited to dine that evening with the *Führer* and the Commander-in-Chief of the *Luftwaffe, Reichsmarschall* Hermann Göring. A greater honour to a young officer not yet 25 years of age could not be imagined.

His euphoria was bruised, however, when at the end of the month he learnt that his elder brother, Joachim, had been arrested by the *Gestapo*. This was the result of a bizarre sequence of events:

In England, a man called Sefton Delmer, an ex-journalist and fluent German speaker, was head of the Black Propaganda department of the secret Political Warfare Executive. The purpose of his department was to dream up and circulate documents and rumours purporting to have emanated from Germany which would cause annoyance or embarrassment to the *Nazis*. He had already had several notable successes.

Werner Mölders was an ace *Luftwaffe* fighter pilot, the first to have achieved 100 victories, who had been killed in a flying accident, in which he was a passenger, in November 1941. His extraordinary record had made him a national hero. Like Helmut Lent, Mölders was a deeply religious man of generous nature who insisted that his captured foes should always be treated with courtesy and respect and often invited them to dine with him.

Most of the Christian denominations in Germany had little time for the *Nazis*, with their obsessive anti-semitism and belief in Aryan superiority, and Delmer recognised an opportunity, using the high esteem in which Mölders was held, to drive the wedge deeper between Church and State. Using forged *Luftwaffe* signal paper, he wrote a carefully constructed letter, claiming to have been written by Mölders before his death, implying, effectively, that his Catholic faith had been more important to his success than his membership of the *Nazi* party. Copies of the letter were dropped in Germany by Bomber Command.

The *Nazis* were understandably furious but soon recognised and exposed the letter as a forgery but not before several clergymen had read the letter out to their congregations. They were immediately arrested by the *Gestapo*, Helmut's brother Joachim included. Helmut had to use his position as a lauded national hero to intervene on Joachim's behalf. His other brother, Werner, also a protestant minister, was to be in trouble with the *Gestapo* the following month for his negative attitude towards the State.

With nine victories to his credit in the month of June, Helmut had good reason to be satisfied and with the short, light nights of summer still to run their course, there should be equally good opportunities ahead in July.

Oberst Werner Mölders, the first Luftwaffe pilot to have achieved 100 victories.

BUNDESARCHIV BILD 183-B12003/JÖLLE/CC-BY-SA 3.0

Chapter 10 – Showdown

RAF Marham, Norfolk, 1800 hrs, 26th July 1942

The Wing Commander was flying with them on this mission so Johnny Stock would, for once, be a true second pilot. While it was obviously an honour to have such a distinguished addition to the crew, it would not be quite the same without Alan Cousens whose ways they knew so well. The regular crew members had honed themselves into such an efficient and predictable unit that flying together was like wearing a pair of old, comfortable slippers.

The two 'vacancies' in their regular crew had been filled at the start of the month: the regular front gunner was now Sergeant Fred Newbound a 31 year-old Yorkshireman who, like most of the others, had enlisted just for the war. Fred came from Harehill, an inner city area of north-east Leeds providing, in the main, housing for workers in the coal mines, brick works and two large textile factories. Fred had enlisted in August 1940 and done his gunnery training but had then been plagued with ill health and had spent much of the next year in and out of the RAF Hospital in Ely. It had not been until 1st June 1942 that he had received an operational posting to No. 115 Squadron at Marham.

Allocated to the crew of Pilot Officer Patterson, Fred made his first operational flight on 5th June in a raid on Emden, followed by three minelaying missions, a further raid on Emden and then two on Bremen. By the end of the month he had therefore been on eight missions whereas most of the men who joined up with him had already completed their first tour. Because of this and the fact that his health was still not 100%, he had tended to become rather introverted and unsure of himself and felt rather outside the clanny coterie of gunners in the Sergeants' Mess. Alec, as Gunnery Leader, soon recognised him as someone who would require special attention; he was potentially a good gunner and Alec decided to take him into his own crew from the beginning of July where he could keep an eye on him while nurturing his ability and self-confidence. Fred had not let him down and was becoming an excellent gunner and was fitting in well with his new colleagues.

Flight Sergeant William Martin Kostyshyn RCAF

The other new member of the crew was the navigator, Flight Sergeant William Martin Kostyshyn RCAF, a Canadian from Melville, a small town in Saskatchewan. The story of the Kostyshyn family was a classic example of the industry and enterprise of immigrant families from the Old World to the New in the 19th and 20th centuries. The Kostyshyns actually originated in the Western Ukraine although William's father, John, was born in Austria to where his father had previously emigrated and was working at the time. John emigrated to North America in 1907 firstly to Webster, Massachusetts and then, with the encouragement of Canadian immigration officials, to Winnipeg where he got a job on the Canadian Pacific Railway. For twelve years he worked hard, for long hours, in a variety of jobs on the railway until, in 1919, he had saved enough to buy a small farm near Goodeve in Saskatchewan. He farmed until 1926 when he bought an hotel and a pool room in Goodeve and subsequently bought and operated hotels and pool rooms in Melville, Waldron and Red Rock, Ontario. John and his wife Mary, who had also emigrated from Austria, had five children and it was their son William who would form the last link in the chain of integration by showing that he was prepared to fight, and if necessary die for, the family's adopted country.

With this crew the Squadron Leader had flown on two previous operations in July, to Bremen on 1st and Duisburg on 22nd. Apart from a partial hang up of their bomb load on the Duisburg raid, both operations had gone quite smoothly. A companion on these two raids, and others, was the aircraft flown by Flight Sergeant Selmer Mooney with gunner Sergeant Margerison, who had flown on occasions with Alec's crew, and navigator Sergeant Bruce. Don Bruce later wrote several excellent pieces about his time with 115 Squadron including a detailed account of this raid.

The coming raid to Hamburg on this night, however, was to be a big one: with over 400 aircraft it was to be a 'maximum effort' operation for all the regular bomber squadrons without involving training and conversion units as had been necessary for the 1,000 raids. Visibility was good and with a huge force of mainly experienced crews it promised to be a notable night and one which the Wing Commander felt he could not miss. Alan Cousens had therefore been stood down for the night.

Frank William Dixon-Wright had been born in 1911 in Devon where his father, Revd. Henry Dixon-Wright, was serving as chaplain to the Royal Naval College, Dartmouth. In this position, Revd. Dixon-Wright had prepared Prince Edward (the future King Edward Vlll and Duke of Windsor) for his Confirmation and in 1910 had been present at the ceremony in Windsor Castle conducted by the Archbishop of Canterbury in front of Queen Alexandra.

Having served in a number of famous Royal Navy ships, including the Royal Yacht, HMS *Medina*, he had been posted to the battleship HMS *Barham* in 1915 which, in the following year, took part in the Battle of Jutland during which he was struck in the spine by a splinter and seriously wounded. He died the next day. It is recorded that he was an eloquent preacher who was praying for victory as he lay dying.

So young Frank was without a father from the age of five and was brought up by his mother, Louisa, until at the age of 13 when he went to the Imperial Service College at Windsor. This was a public school principally for the education of future service officers – the old 'Westward Ho!' where Rudyard Kipling was educated.

From here Frank went to the RAF College Cranwell from where in 1931, aged 20, he passed out and was commissioned as a Pilot Officer. While serving with No. 98 Squadron in 1941 he had been awarded the Distinguished Flying Cross 'For gallantry in flying operations against enemy warships at Brest including the *Gneisnau*, *Scharnhorst* and *Prince Eugen*.' In the same year he was promoted to Temporary Wing Commander and on 20th May 1942 had been appointed as Commanding Officer of No. 115 Squadron at Marham. He was a young and very 'hands-on' commander who flew on operations whenever he could and was popular with officers and men alike.

During the morning of 26th July the airfield at Marham had been a hive of activity: riggers and engine fitters swarmed all over the aircraft which were parked on their dispersals preparing them for the night's operation; inside the planes wireless and instrument technicians checked and replaced pieces of equipment; convoys of motor tractors, pulling strings of trailers carrying high explosive and incendiary bombs, zig-zagged acrosss the airfield between the bomb stores and the dispersals; teams of armourers loaded the bombs into the open bomb bays while others loaded the machine gun rounds into their belts and delivered them to the magazines in the front and rear turrets. The aircraft must all be loaded up and 100% ready before zero hour when the crews would arrive and take them over. In another part of the airfield meteorologists launched weather balloons and took readings to enable them to give the crews the most accurate and up-to-date weather predictions possible for their impending mission.

The Wing Commander called for the briefing at 1430 and introduced it himself. The target was Hamburg he told the assembled crews and it was to be a 'maximum effort' raid with over 400 aircraft. There would be 14 aircraft from 115 Squadron – 8 from 'A' Flight and 6 from 'B' – take off would be from 2300. Squadron Leader Cousens then briefed the 72 crew members on the target showing them the latest aerial photographs of Hamburg and a map of possible approaches. Detailed target maps would be handed out to navigators after the briefing. Then followed briefings on their bomb loads, on signals and call signs for the wireless operators and, finally, a weather briefing by the station meteorologist. Navigators then consulted with pilots, studying the maps together and discussing their course and approach to the target. Alec made himself available to the other gunners in the squadron and answered questions from some of the less experienced on technicalities and procedures.

The crews spent the rest of the afternoon in their messes trying to relax or snatch some last minute sleep; it would be a long night and they must be alert throughout it, but sleep did not come easily and the waiting was tedious – all they wanted now was to get on with the job. A tense evening meal with conversation strained or rather over-jocular until 2100 arrived and they made their way to the crew room to don their flying gear.

The crew room was thick with smoke, in the days when everybody smoked, many of them pipes, and noisy with friendly banter between rival crews. This bonhomie helped to ease the nervous tension which always existed at this stage of every operation. At last the transport to take the crews

Aircrew of a Wellington bomber board their aircraft at its dispersal at the start of an operation.

to their aircraft began arriving. The first lorry took the crews of the four aircraft which would take off first – 'F-FOX', Pilot Officer Douglas Rhode, 'D-DOG', Pilot Officer D Fry, 'R-ROGER', Sergeant C Glauser and 'X-XRAY', Sergeant Walter Norrington from Hove in Sussex who at 18 years of age was the youngest aircraft captain on the operation. The crew of 'G-GEORGE', Alec's aircraft, was in the second lorry together with the crews of 'V-VICTOR', Pilot Officer J Berry, 'L-LOVE', Sergeant Jim Howells, a New Zealander, and 'K-KING', Sergeant B Fereday. As the lorry drove round delivering each crew to its dispersal the banter continued and as each of them left the lorry they were sent off with shouts of good luck and good natured taunts from their comrades.

'G-GEORGE' stood waiting for her aircrew on the dispersal, massive and menacing, with members of the ground crew bustling about finishing off last minute preparations; the ladder to the crew hatch in her belly was in place and an instrument technician emerged – the last of the ground crew to leave the aircraft. Before climbing into the plane the crew performed the ritual of relieving themselves on the tail wheel which they considered essential for their good luck although the practice was frowned upon by authority. It was, in fact, quite sensible to take advantage of this last opportunity: there was a little Elsan chemical lavatory on board but often crew members were unable to leave their stations and had to rely upon a trusty milk bottle.

Alec scrambled through the narrow fuselage of the bomber and installed himself in the rear turret as he had done so many times before. He had written to Nessie the previous day telling her that he would be getting a long leave in September, and promising that they would go away somewhere for a few days, and again singing the praises of Alan Cousens:

> **"I've been getting the trips in and can now claim to have done 44 . . . flying with a person as conscientious as S/L Cousens you have the satisfaction of knowing that you get to the target and light the way for the other lads. He certainly is a grand captain, something like old Neil – bags of determination and guts."**

He also commented on the news Nessie had been giving him of some of his Edinburgh friends who were serving in the army:

> **"I'm glad Jimmy Collins is getting on alright, he's a nice laddie. Too bad Alan Reid is fed up. Wait till they open up the Second Front and the 'Brownies' will be fed up in a different way!"**

At 2230 pilots began starting up in the dispersals and the throb of the great Hercules engines invaded every corner of the airfield. Alec completed his pre-takeoff routines and settled back in the cramped quarters he had come to know so well. Fred Newbound did the same in the front turret, George Whittaker checked over his wireless equipment, William Kostyshyn opened out his chart on the navigator's table and began to mark up the route and Johnny Stock assisted the Wing Commander with the pre-take-off checks in the cockpit.

RAF OFFICIAL PHOTOGRAPHER F/O FORWARD

Wellington X3662 of 115 Squadron flown by 18 year-old Pilot Officer Ivor Slade from Hemel Hempstead.

The captain taxied to the runway head and at 2250 the green Aldis flash was received and they were ready for take-off. With a heavy load of bombs and fuel the captain decided upon a take-off which involved forcing the tail of the aircraft off the ground before the run commenced. With his brakes hard on he opened the throttles wider and wider until Alec in his turret rose up from the ground; the brakes were then released and 'G-GEORGE' leaped forward like a racehorse from the starting gate. As they lifted off the runway at 2352 Pilot Officer Douglas Rhode in 'F-FREDDIE' behind them had already started his run. The roar of engines at full power as the aircraft took off one after the other resounded throughout the surrounding countryside and neighbouring villages telling the inhabitants that another great strike at the enemy was under way.

The last of the fourteen aircraft of 115 Squadron, 'W-WILLIAM' flown by Sergeant D McKee, left the ground at 2327; the whole takeoff had been completed in 35 minutes. Once they were over the North Sea 'R-ROGER' developed engine trouble and the captain, Sergeant C Glauser, decided they must turn back and return to Marham with their bombs. The rest of the squadron, having tested their guns, settled down on an easterly course heading for the Dutch coast and Hamburg.

* * * * *

At the *Luftwaffe* airfield at Leeuwarden, Sunday 26th July 1942 had been much the same as any other Sunday. Being a nightfighter station, the aircrews were left very much to their own devices during the day except for when they were required to flight test aircraft or undertake routine training exercises. Helmut Lent, however, was finding that, with his administrative duties as *Gruppenkommandeur,* his days were now just as busy as his nights.

It was with some relief, therefore, that he finished his last bit of paperwork for the day and made his way to the officers' mess for a meal before the night's operations. After this he joined the other pilots in the crewroom where they would await the nightly call to arms.

On 1st January Helmut had been promoted to *Hauptmann* and, at 23 years 6 months, he was the youngest *Gruppenkomandeur* in the *Nachtjagd.* Normally it would have taken three years in the rank of *Oberleutnant* before promotion to *Hauptmann*. He had also acquired added responsibilities: two new *staffels* each comprising a small detachment under the command of an experienced nightfighter had been established at Bergen aan Zee on the Dutch coast and at Wittmundhafen near Wilhelmshaven. These were commanded respectively by *Prinz* Egmont zur Lippe-Weissenfeld and Rudolf Schoenert each with a formidable number of kills to his credit.

By now the *Luftwaffe* had developed its nightfighter control procedures into a pretty finely-honed art: the coastline and hinterland across which the bomber streams must pass on their way to and from their targets was divided into *Räumes* or zones *(see page 250)*. Each zone had a *Freya* radar installation, a long-range system which had been in service for some time. This radar would detect and track the incoming stream and alert the nightfighters to scramble and

Oberleutnant Prinz Egmont zur Lippe-Weissenfeld.

Oberleutnant Rudolf Schoenert.

WWW.NACHTJAEGERSPODEN.DE

await arrival of the bombers. In the centre of each zone was the radio beacon on which pilots could home and around which they would circle as they waited for more detailed information. This came from another ground-based radar known as the 'Red' *Würzburg* which took over from the *Freya* once the aircraft were in the zone and would guide an individual nightfighter to an individual target. The final link in the procedure was a second *Würzburg* radar, known as the 'Green' *Würzburg,* which would be focussed on the nightfighter enabling the ground controller to guide the night hunter directly to its prey.

Helmut Lent had won two victories so far in July, the first on 3rd when he intercepted a Wellington of 301 Squadron over Assen, south-east of Leeuwarden; it had been one of thirteen RAF aircraft lost in the major raid on Bremen in which Alec had also taken part. Helmut's second kill was on 9th, another Wellington, this time of 75 Squadron, which was taking part in another major raid on Wilhelmshaven. He shot it down over Rottumeroog a small uninhabited island in the West Frisian group off the Dutch coast, south-west of Borkum.

The long periods of waiting in the crewroom were spent reading, smoking, playing cards and chatting with comrades. Occasionally tactics would be discussed and, with the prospect of imminent action, the adrenalin would be running high precluding any chance of a last minute nap before the summons.

The night of 26th July had been much the same as any other until, shortly after midnight, the telephone rang; conversation stopped short and all eyes focussed on the *Kommandeur* as he picked it up. The message was brief and to the point – the 'Tommies' were on their way and it was time to get into flying kit and await further instructions. Twenty minutes later it rang again and the keyed-up airmen were on their feet and making for the door even before they received the feverishly-awaited command to 'Go'.

Figures raced across the crewroom road as fast as their bulky flying kit would allow, the more athletic of them taking a regularly used short cut which involved jumping over a wire fence to get to their aircraft with the minimum of delay. Helmut's ground crew were waiting for him beside his black bf110; one man dropped his parachute over his shoulders and fastened the elastic straps; another assisted him into the cramped cockpit as his *Funker*, Walter Kubisch, settled himself in his seat behind and back-to-back to the pilot; the canopy closed over their heads as the port engine sprang into life to be quickly followed by the starboard one.

Helmut opened the throttles and the two Daimler-Benz V-12 engines gave up their combined 2,200 horse power as the aircraft raced along the runway which had been built over rubble from the ruins of the City of Rotterdam destroyed by the *Luftwaffe* in May 1940. Helmut eased back on the joystick and the aircraft lifted off and commenced its climb to operational height.

It was soon apparent to aircrew and ground controllers alike that the RAF were in considerable strength; the *Freya* radar had detected a great concentration of several hundred aircraft approaching the coast and it was feared that this could be another of Harris's 1,000 bomber raids which had caused such devastation in Cologne on 31st May. The destructive power of these massed formations was awesome but, from the nightfighters' point of view, the pickings were prodigious. Helmut positioned himself close to the beacon for his *Räume* and awaited instructions.

Messerschmitt Bf110

RAF BATTLE OF BRITAIN CAMPAIGN DIARIES

Though the bomber stream was tightly packed, with more than 400 aircraft it was improbable that any crew would sight a plane from their own squadron during the whole operation. There was, however, a feeling of fellowship as they could see other bombers to left, right, above and below them in their three-dimensional world, all heading on the same course and speed with the same objective in mind. Having passed unscathed through the usual coastal flak and nightfighter zones, the aircraft of 115 Squadron approached the outskirts of Hamburg. Alec's plane, 'G-GEORGE', with the most senior captain and the most experienced crew was in the van to mark the target and, in accordance with Harris's multi-level plan, the squadron was to bomb at different heights ranging from 13,000 feet to 16,000 feet in 500 feet increments. The weather was fair with a light south-west wind and moderate visibility; all the variable factors upon which a raid could succeed or fail augured well for a successful attack.

Wing Commander Dixon-Wright in 'G-GEORGE' dropped his bombs from 13,000 feet and observed a considerable conflagration below before he turned and headed for home. 'K-KING', flown by Sergeant B Fereday, bombed at the lowest level of 12,000 feet and was one of three aircraft in the squadron to carry a 4,000 lb bomb. This huge bomb had been designed for the new generation of heavy, four-engined bombers and to accommodate it in a Wellington meant removal of the bomb doors, which reduced the speed of the aircraft and, more importantly, required the removal of most of the flotation bags which were designed to keep the aircraft afloat in the event of a ditching. Fereday unloaded his great bomb and turned for home.

'V-VICTOR', Pilot Officer J D Berry, bombed from 13,000 feet, took two photographs and turned for home closely followed by 'W-WILLIAM', Sergeant D McKee, 'Q-QUEEN', Pilot Officer H G A'Court and 'L-LOVE', Sergeant L Howells, the New Zealander whose first operation this was in command having previously flown only five missions as a second pilot. Anxious to bring back a good photograph, Sergeant Howells lingered a little too long over the target and was hit by flak which damaged his port engine. This caused violent vibration which threatened to shake the whole aircraft apart leaving Howells with no alternative but to shut down the engine and head for home.

The next most senior officer in the squadron's contingent, Squadron Leader T L Sandes flying 'N-NAN', bombed from 14,500 feet and noted that the whole city appeared to be ablaze. 'D-DOG', Pilot Officer A D Fry, 'Y-YOKE', Sergeant W Norrington, and 'B-BAKER', Sergeant J B Smith, dropped their bombs from 15,000 feet close to the aiming point.

On the north bank of the River Elbe, opposite the main docks, two artificial lakes, the Binnenalster and the larger Aussenalster were a great aid to airmen in fixing their position over the city of Hamburg. Pilot Officer G Grimston in 'H-HOW' dropped his bombs from 15,500 feet one mile south of the Binnenalster and noted that there were several fires raging south of the lakes. Pilot Officer D O Rhode in 'F-FOX' also bombed from 15,500 and observed the aiming point enveloped with enormous fires. At the highest level of 16,000 feet, Flight Sergeant J Newman in 'X-XRAY' dropped his bombs slightly east of the aiming point, took one photograph then turned for home.

The 13 aircraft of 115 Squadron (the 14th, 'R-ROGER', having turned back early with engine trouble), survived the intensive flak over Hamburg and were heading back for the coast on their return journey. The only casualty so far was 'L-LOVE' which, with its port engine disabled was losing height rapidly. Sergeant Howells realised he would not make it home but managed to cross the German coast and reconciled himself to an imminent ditching in the North Sea which seemed to offer a better chance of survival than a crash landing in Germany. He warned his crew to prepare for ditching.

'K-KING' as it approached the coast received a very near miss from the ground fire which disabled the aircraft's electrical and hydraulic systems. The undercarriage dropped down, both gun turrets were rendered inoperative and the navigation equipment, including the compass, were put out of use. Sergeant K Shoesmith, the rear gunner, and Sergeant G Clerides, the W/T operator, were both wounded and the drag of the lowered undercarriage added to that of the missing bomb doors caused Sergeant Fereday to temporarily lose control and the aircraft went into a steep dive. Sergeant Clerides, semi conscious and getting no response from his intercom, believed that the rest of the crew had baled out and, as he thought, followed them.

A flight of Wellington bombers.

Fereday, however, managed to regain control and with no W/T operator, a wounded gunner and no electrical equipment working, headed for what he believed to be the direction of the coast only to realise that he had been flying in the wrong direction and was approaching the suburbs of Hamburg again. He turned around and without a compass or any navigational aids attempted to fly on a west-south-westerly course. Losing height all the time due to the excessive drag Fereday coaxed the aircraft over the coast and out across the North Sea in what he hoped was roughly the right direction for home. But luck was not with them and at about 1,500 feet both engines cut out and defied all attempts to restart them. Sergeant Fereday shouted at the top of his voice to his remaining crew members to prepare for ditching.

Sergeant Cleredes meanwhile, who had jumped out, landed near Bremen and was immediately surrounded by a hostile mob. Cleredes was a Greek Cypriot and seeing his swarthy Eastern Mediterranean features and suspecting that he was jewish, the mob closed in on him with taunts of *"Juden, Juden"* and started to beat him up while rifling his pockets and equipment at the same time. Fortunately for him, a *Luftwaffe* patrol intervened and took him to a hospital in Bremen where he was taken straight into the theatre for an operation on his wounded leg.

Sergeant Smith in 'B-BAKER' delivered his bombs satisfactorily on the target but, on his way home, received a direct hit on his port engine from an anti-aircraft battery near Wilhelmshaven. Smith shut down the engine and battled with his controls to offset the swing to port caused by the starboard engine; the front gunner, Sergeant Fawcus, came back and helped him take the strain by holding the rudder bar back for him but, despite both their efforts, the plane was steadily losing height. Although still under fire from the ground they managed to cross the German coast without further damage but there was no chance of being able to keep the plane airborne for much longer and Sergeant Smith ordered his crew to prepare for ditching.

As the crew of 'L-LOVE' prepared for ditching, Sergeant W Walker, the navigator, collected the Verey pistol and cartridges but had them torn from his hand when the aircraft hit the water. They managed to launch their dinghy and all clamber into it but they then discovered that, as well as having lost their Verey pistol, all the emergency flares in the dinghy had perished and were unuseable. Sergeants J Howells, W Walker, W Shepherd, W Waite and C Lindridge were adrift in the North Sea without any means of attracting the attention of passing ships or aircraft.

Sergeant Fereday managed to nurse 'K-KING' across the German coast in spite of being without hydraulic or electrical power and the excessive drag caused by the lowered undercarriage and absence of bomb doors. When the lowered undercarriage hit the water it tipped the bomber onto its nose flinging the crew and all loose equipment violently forward. They all managed to get out of the aircraft only to find that their dinghy was riddled with holes from shrapnel and would hold no air. A wooden dais upon which crew members would stand when using the astro dome had floated out of the sinking aircraft and the airmen managed to swim to it and hold on to it.

Sergeant Kelvin Hewer Shoesmith, the 21 year-old Australian rear gunner, had been wounded in his side and his life jacket had been pierced by shrapnel. He was clearly in distress and Sergeant Harry Lindley, the Navigator, kept blowing up his life jacket to keep him afloat. But he must have been more seriously wounded than anyone realised and soon lost consciousness; despite their efforts, he lost his grip and floated away. Next to go was Sergeant Frank Skelley, the 19 year-old WT operator and front gunner from Manchester. He was unable to hold on any longer and the remaining two were now too weak to assist him. He too floated away.

As Sergeant Glafkos Cleredes had already baled out over Germany, this left just Fereday and Lindley, exhausted and already beginning to suffer from exposure, clinging desperately onto the wooden dais and praying for a miracle.

Sergeant Jim Smith and his crew in 'B-BAKER' were perhaps the most fortunate. As they descended towards the sea Smith cut his starboard engine and glided down to a textbook belly ditching made possible by the fact that the moon emerged from cloud and flooded the sea with light at exactly the right time for them. Sergeant Jim Smith, Pilot Officer W D'Ath the Navigator, and Sergeants J French, L Harcus and W Frizzel, WT Operator, Front Gunner and Rear Gunner respectively, evacuated the aircraft in a calm and orderly fashion and watched 'B-BAKER' sink from the safety of their life raft. This was the third of three aircraft from 'A' Flight, 115 Squadron, whose crews were adrift in the North Sea and praying that they would be spotted and rescued.

Helmut Lent had had no luck with the tightly packed, incoming bomber stream and was waiting for the returning aircraft which he knew would be more scattered and vulnerable as they crossed the coast homeward bound. At 0235 he spotted a four-engined bomber which turned out to be a Halifax of 102 Squadron from Topcliffe which had converted to the heavy bomber earlier in the year. He sent it flaming into the sea. Just four minutes later, at 0239, he intercepted 'G-GEORGE', Wing Commander Dixon-Wright's Wellington.

He destroyed it with its entire crew. It was Helmut Lent's 51st kill.

Nobody will ever know the exact circumstances of this engagement: did he attack from above, below, from front, rear or flank? Did Alec ever get a chance to return his fire or was he the first to be killed by the deadly cannon fire from Helmut's *Zerstorer*? Indeed, was the attacker even spotted or did death come instantly and unexpectedly? As the visibility was good, it is very probable that he used an attack technique known as *von hinten unten*, meaning 'from behind and below', which was being adopted increasingly by nightfighter pilots with considerable success. The nightfighter would creep up slowly in a gentle climb from below and behind the bomber so its black fuselage was well camouflaged against the dark ground below. The pilot would then hope to kill the rear gunner with his first burst so he could finish the job from behind without returning fire. This approach was not effective, of course, when the aircraft were operating above low cloud which made the attackers very visible against the white background. We shall never know exactly what happened but an account of one of Helmut Lent's earlier victories, which may have been similar, was recorded by Josef Kreutz, an official German war correspondent. In an article entitled: 'Victory in the Night Sky' Kreutz wrote:

> **". . . A British bomber has crossed the flight path of the searching night fighter. The range is growing shorter and shorter. Will the enemy crew see the fighter? But there is not a single shot. The Tommy is now within attacking range. The guns are loaded and set to 'Fire'. One press on the button and all hell will be let loose. But still the *Eichenlaubträger* holds back. He wants the first attack to blow the enemy to pieces. He wants to make quite certain that his target is right in his sights. Another slight adjustment of position – then it is time. The cannon hammer out in short bursts, then there comes the lighter rattle of the machine-guns. His aim is good! A flurry of bright fragments from the aircraft swirls through the air and there are already flames emerging from the vast fuselage of the British bomber. *Hauptmann* Lent pulls his aircraft away . . . all around night turns to day. Fragments fly around like flaming torches . . . the instantaneous destructive effect of the German night fighter's attack gave the enemy crew no chance of escape."**

The body of Pilot Officer George Whittaker DFM, the W/T operator, was later washed up on a Heligoland beach and was the only member of Alec's crew to be recovered. He is now buried in one of the Commonwealth War Graves Commission areas of Hamburg Cemetery.

In Memory of

Pilot Officer

Alexander Johnston Stewart Ollar

D F M

120067, 115 Sqdn., Royal Air Force Volunteer Reserve who died on 27 July 1942 Age 31

Son of Stewart Ollar and of Ethel Gertrude Ollar (nee Sherwood); husband of Agnes McNeil Ollar (nee Gilzean).

Remembered with Honour
Runnymede Memorial

Commemorated in perpetuity by
the Commonwealth War Graves Commission

Date	Hour	Aircraft Type and No.	Pilot	Duty
2-7-42	2316	WELLINGTON X3471	S/LDR COUSENS, D.F.C. P/O STOCK	AIR GUNNER
13·7·42	1100	WELLINGTON X3412	P/O STOCK	AIR GUNNER
13-7-42	1500	WELLINGTON X3412	P/O STOCK	AIR GUNNER
17-7-42	1145	WELLINGTON BJ615	P/O STOCK	AIR GUNNER
19-7-42	1420	WELLINGTON BJ615	W/C DIXON-WRIGHT P/O STOCK	AIR GUNNER
21.7.42		G	P/O STOCK	AIR GUNNER
23·7·42		G	P/O STOCK	AIR GUNNER
23.7 42		G	P/O STOCK	AIR GUNNER
26.7 42		G	W/C DIXON-WRIGHT P/O STOCK	AIR GUNNER
COMMANDING A - FLIGHT. No. 115 SQUADRON.			L Rhode P/O. S/LR	

| Time carried forward :— | 344·05 | 231·55 |

REMARKS (including results of bombing, gunnery, exercises, etc.)	Flying Times	
	Day	Night
OPERATIONS - BREMEN		5·10
AIR TEST	·20	
NORTHOLT & RETURN	1·10	
AIR TO SEA FIRING	1·00	
NORTHOLT & RETURN	1·30	
AIR TEST	40	
LOCAL & AIR/SEA FIRING	1·15	
OPS.		3·45
OPS FAILED TO RETURN		
TOTAL TIME ...		

DEATH PRESUMED

CENTRAL DEPOSITARY
JUL 1946
ROYAL AIR FORCE

Chapter 11 – High Noon of the Nachtjagd

All three of the 115 Squadron crews who had ditched in the North Sea in the early hours of 27th July 1942 were rescued by the Norderney *Seenotgruppe*. This was the *Luftwaffe* air-sea rescue service based on Norderney, one of the East Frisian Islands off the coast of Germany. Their white-painted Dornier Do24 flying boats with Red Cross markings constantly patrolled the area and were responsible for saving the lives of many hundreds of RAF airmen.

Sergeants Fereday and Lindley, after nearly six hours clinging to their wooden dais, were nearly at the end of their endurance when Fereday saw the welcome sight of the white Dornier landing in the sea close to them. Lindley was already unconscious and remembered nothing of the rescue afterwards. The German crewmen also recovered the bodies of Kelvin Shoesmith and Frank Skelley and, having confirmed that both were dead, returned their bodies to the sea. Shoesmith was later washed up on the coast of Denmark and is buried at Esbjerg Cemetery. Skelley's body was washed ashore on the Dutch coast and is buried on Texel.

Sergeant Howells and the crew of 'L-LOVE', although safely in their dinghy, were at a great disadvantage without any means to attract the attention of rescuers. Over the next three days several British aircraft passed overhead but did not spot them until, on the third day, a Dornier of the Norderney *Seenotgruppe* picked them up and took them prisoner.

Sergeant Smith and his crew were the most fortunate: having made a textbook belly landing and evacuation of 'B-BAKER' at 0300, they had only to wait in their dinghy until 0930 before being spotted, picked up and taken into captivity.

Out of 403 British aircraft on the raid, 29 were lost including the four from 115 Squadron. Squadron Leader Cousens was appalled to learn that he had lost half the strength of his 'A' Flight in just one night, including his own 'personal' crew. Of the 29 bombers destroyed, 8 were victims of the *Nachtjagt* and, as usual, Helmut Lent's *Gruppe* II./NJG 2 were the most successful with seven kills to its credit including the two accounted for by Lent himself.

Dornier Do24 flying boat of the type used by the Norderney Seenogruppe which saved the lives of hundreds of RAF aircrew.

The damage done to Hamburg was heavy and extensive. The city fire brigade was called out to about 800 fires, with over 500 being classified as 'major', and for the first time they had to call for reinforcements from other areas. More than 5,000 houses were damaged with 823 completely destroyed and 14,000 people made homeless. Over 1,000 people were injured and 337 killed. Within the context of the RAF's defined objectives, the raid had been a resounding success though their own toll, at 7% of the force employed, was high.

On the evening of the 27th Nessie was devastated to receive the telegram that every wife and mother dreaded advising her that Alec was reported missing.

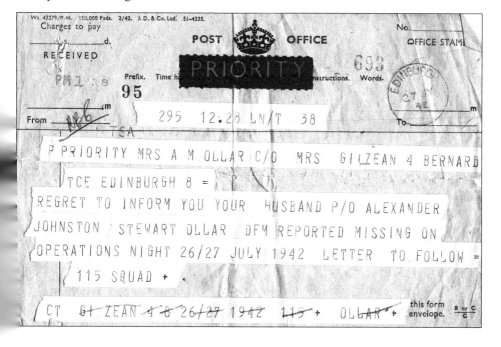

R.A.F. Masham.

Thursday.

Dear Mrs. Ollar,

It is with the deepest regret that I have to confirm that your husband has been reported missing.

As you probably know he was a member of my crew. On the night in question I was stood down & the Wing-Commander took the crew out. The crew was the finest bunches of boys it has ever been my lot to fly with, in the air, they were absolutely perfect at their job.

Alec, as I have said to many people again & again was quite the finest rear gunner I have ever flown with, & I have flown with many, his control & behaviour in the air was an example to all, in fact I used to take rear-gunners of other crews, out with me to help me out.

Again please accept my deepest regrets.

Yours sincerely,
A. Cousens.

This was followed the next day by a hand written letter from Alan Cousens who, with the loss of Frank Dixon-Wright, had been promoted to acting Wing Commander:

RAF Marham

Monday

Dear Mrs Ollar,
      It is with the deepest regret that I have to confirm that your husband has been reported missing.

      As you probably know he was a member of my crew. On the night in question I was stood down and the Wing-Commander took the crew over.

      The crew was the finest bunch of boys it has ever been my lot to fly with, in the air, they were absolutely perfect at their job.

      Alec, as I have said to many people again and again was quite the finest rear gunner I have ever flown with, and I have flown with many, his control and behaviour in the air was an example to all, in fact I used to take rear-gunners of other crews out with me in order to learn the way things should be done.

      We heard nothing at all from them after take-off and so we can only hope that they may have managed to get out, should I get any news I will let you know immediately.

      I have now taken over the Squadron I only wish I had the boys with me to help me out.

      Again please accept my deepest regrets.
      Yours sincerely,
      A. Cousens, w/c

There had seemed little point in Nessie paying out rent and living alone in their flat in Edinburgh when Alec was away and, earlier in the year, they had decided that she should give up the flat and move back in with her parents in Bernard Terrace. It was very fortunate that during this emotional crisis in her life she had the support of her parents close at hand.

Understandably, she could not accept that Alec was dead. She wondered if any of the other aircraft had seen his plane after the raid and convinced herself that thay may have developed engine trouble and ditched in the sea. She wrote to Alan Cousens asking if he had any further news. She told him how much Alec had enjoyed his job and how pleased he was to be in his crew. The Wing Commander replied immediately:

> **Thank you for your letter. I am afraid I cannot give you any concrete news. Nothing was heard from the aircraft after take off, the possibility of other crews having seen their particular aircraft in the target area is remote as we lost other aircraft that night.**
>
> **I think it is very doubtful that they went down in the sea due to engine trouble, as we would have heard from them. The operator Whittaker was a first-class man at his job and he would have got some message through.**
>
> **I am terribly glad that Alec was happy in the crew, I will let you have the addresses of the other permanent members of the crew. You can rely on me to let you know any news that I might hear immediately. Please write to me at any time if you feel you want to as I would like to keep in touch with the relatives of my crew as I feel someday that we will all get together again.**
>
> **The Air Ministry will let you have any news they hear, via the Squadron. The crew were:**
>
> **P/O Johnny Stock (Pilot), (mother) Mrs F H Stock, Wellington Hotel, Boscastle, North Cornwall**
>
> **P/O George Whittaker (W/Op), (mother) Mrs Whittaker, The Knells, Houghton, Carlisle, Cumberland**
>
> **Again all my hopes and wishes are with you.**

you can rely on me to let you
know any news that I might hear,
immeadiately, please write to me
at any time if you feel you want
to .... like to keep in
You ....

R.A.F. ....
Tuesday

Dear Mrs ......,

Thank you for your letter,
I am afraid I cannot give you
any concrete news.

Nothing we heard from the aircraft
after take off, the possibility of
this crew having seen their particular
aircraft in the ...... area is remote
as were ...... other aircraft that night.
I think it ...... very doubtful that
they went down in the sea due
to engine trouble, as we would
have heard from them, the operator
Whittaker was a first-class man at
his job & he would have got some
message through.

I am terribly glad that Alec
was happy in the crew, I will let
you have the address of the other
that ...... those of the rest crew who
are took ...... not returned.

After a long leave in August, Helmut Lent destroyed his first Lancaster bomber at 0250 on 5th September 1942 to be followed by a further four kills by the end of the year, three of which were *viermots* as the Germans called the four-engined heavies. A reorganisation of the *nachtjagd* structure put Lent in command of IV./NJG 1 from 1st October and, returning from Christmas leave he learnt that he had been promoted from *Hauptmann* to *Major*, a very unusual honour for an officer aged only 24.

The losses inflicted by Bomber Command from the nightfighters were becoming increasingly serious: during the three-month period June to August 1942, 531 RAF bombers had been lost of which 349 were accounted for by the *Nachtjagd*. The nature of the bombing offensive was changing in a number of ways. Firstly, both sides were struggling to get ahead of the other in the new science of electronic warfare. Britain had a setback when the Germans discovered how to jam their *Gee* direction-finding equipment but the new *Oboe*, an extremely accurate target location system, had been in limited use since early 1942 and by the end of the year was being fitted in some operational aircraft including the Mosquito, the new, fast, muti-role precision bomber. At the same time *H2S*, the first ground-scanning radar was coming on stream and the accuracy of RAF navigation and target location was transformed, even in zero visibility conditions.

The next innovation was the introduction of the Pathfinder Force (PFF) where very experienced crews, in aircraft equipped with H2S, would precede the main bomber stream to locate and mark the target with flares. This, effectively, was the formalisation of a system which was already coming into use at the discretion of individual squadrons. Initially there were five Pathfinder squadrons but in January 1943 they were expanded to form a Group and, ultimately, there were nineteen PFF squadrons. By the middle of the year, two Pathfinder squadrons, 105 and 139, equipped with Mosquitos, which were proving ideal for pathfinder duties, joined 115 Squadron at Marham.

The last, and perhaps the most important, innovation was the arrival of the United States Army Air Force. The United States had officially entered the war on 7th December 1941 and two months later a new force

Boeing B17 Flying Fortress

designated VIII Bomber Command (VIII BC), later to become the US 8th Air Force, established itself in England. It was equipped with two four-engined heavy bombers – the Boeing B17 Flying Fortress and Consolidated B24 Liberator both of which were to play a major part in the ongoing bomber offensive. The Liberator was the newer design with greater speed, bomb load and operational ceiling, but the older Flying Fortress was more stable and easier to fly and was generally preferred by crews. On 4th July 1942, six B17 Flying Fortresses made the first VIII BC operational flight when, accompanied by six RAF bombers, they attacked *Luftwaffe* airfields in Holland. Regular operations commenced on 17th August when twelve B17s attacked the marshalling yards at Rouen.

Consolidated B24 Liberator

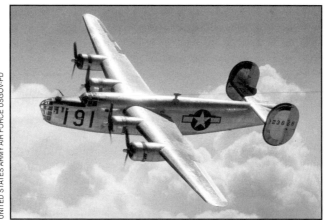

A Norden bomb sight preserved at the 100th Bomb Group USAAF Memorial Museum on the site of the former RAF Thorpe Abbotts, near Diss, Norfolk.

The intention was that the Americans would undertake high altitude, daytime, precision bombing using the new gyro-stabilised Norden bomb sight. Their targets initially were to be enemy installations and shipping in the occupied French Channel ports but in January 1943 the Casablanca Conference agreed a joint strategy with the RAF, the 'Combined Bombing Offensive', under which the enemy would be subjected to round-the-clock attack – by the Americans during the day and the British at night.

On 4th February a force of B17s on a raid to the Ruhr was intercepted by eight bf110s of IV./NJG 1. Helmut Lent was on leave at the time but the men of his *Gruppe* acquitted themselves well. Led by *Oberleutnant* Hans-Joachim Jabs, they very soon realised that the heavily armoured Flying Fortress with its 13, big half-inch Browning machine guns, would be a harder nut to crack than the lighter armed RAF bombers to which they were accustomed. Nevertheless, they managed to shoot down three B17s though all eight of their Messerschmitts sustained damage and two were compelled to crash land. On 26th, Jabs led twelve of the *Gruppe's* planes against a force of B24 Liberators returning from a raid on Emden. Two were shot down but at the cost of one bf110 flown by *Oberleutnant* Ludwig Becker, a legendary nightfighter pilot with 44 kills to his credit.

Oberleutnant Hans-Joachim Jabs, a close friend of Helmut Lent who commanded IV./NJG 1 in his absence.

Lent returned from leave the next day to learn that, in addition to their baptism of fire with the Americans, the *Gruppe* had despatched 13 RAF bombers during his absence.

Helmut was soon back on form with four victories in March including two Halifaxes within 14 minutes of each other on the night of the 5th (of which one was later found to have been a Lancaster – the two types could easily be confused especially at night). Then on 20th April he became the first nightfighter pilot to shoot down a Mosquito. His victim was a marauder from 410 (RCAF) Squadron of Fighter Command flown by Warrant Officer William Reddie RCAF. These aircraft were tasked with patrolling in the *Nachtjagd* zones to try and reduce the number of nightfighters preying on the bomber streams. In this case the hunter became the hunted and the bodies of WO Reddie and his observer, 21 year-old RAFVR Sergeant Ken Evans, were never found. It was a remarkable achievement as the Mosquito could outperform the bf110 in almost every respect and it is an enduring example of Lent's superb airmanship.

On 5th March 1943 Bomber Command embarked upon a massive 5-month offensive against the concentration of industrial cities and installations in the Ruhr which would later be called 'The Battle of the Ruhr'. The destruction and setbacks inflicted on German heavy industry, including steelworks and synthetic oil plants, were enormous and so were Bomber Command's losses. Of the 43 major raids during the 5-month period, 28 were to the Ruhr, or 'Happy Valley' as it was known to the crews. Around 1,000 British bombers were lost and between 5,500 and 6,000 aircrew. Of these losses about 70% were accounted for by the *Nachtjagd* which by now had a total strength of 550 aircraft.

The night of 4th/5th May saw the first major attack on Dortmund: of the 596 bombers in the raid, 31 were shot down and a further 7 crashed in bad weather. German nightfighters accounted for 22 of the 31 losses and 12 of these were claimed by Lent's *Gruppe*. Lent himself destroyed two Stirlings just after midnight within 10 minutes of each other. This brought his total of night kills to 60 and that of IV./NJG 1 to 300.

On 22nd June the USAAF undertook its first major, deep penetration raid into Germany with a raid by 235 B17s on the Hüls oil refinery and synthetic rubber plant. The damage they inflicted halted the production of aircraft tyres for six months. Sixteen American aircraft were lost and 170 were damaged and on the same evening Bomber Command launched a 557-aircraft raid on Mülheim in which 35 aircraft were lost. The pressure on Germany's heartland was unrelenting.

The end of 'The Battle of the Ruhr' marked the beginning of the next major offensive 'The Battle of Hamburg'. This was an intense, maximum effort campaign with four major night raids, each of nearly 800 aircraft, conducted between 24th July and 3rd August. The RAF force included Canadian and Australian squadrons and the USAAF undertook two daylight raids on 26th and 27th.

On the night of 24th/25th the RAF used 'Window' for the first time. This was little strips of foil-backed paper which were released in large quantities on the approach to, and over, the target area. This confused the German radar systems and dramatically reduced the effectiveness of their nightfighters and anti-aircraft batteries. Of 791 aircraft that night, the RAF lost 12 – 1.5% of the force compared with the 5% to which Bomber Command had become reconciled.

In the whole operation the RAF lost 87 aircraft and the USAAF 22 but the damage done to the City of Hamburg was devastating. Codenamed 'Operation Gomorrah' it also became known as 'Germany's Hiroshima'; a period of dry weather had preceded the raid and the bombing on 27th/28th caused a horrific firestorm which set the whole city ablaze. The superheated air rising created violent winds at ground level as cold air rushed in to replace it; the oxygen fed the flames further, asphalt on the roads caught fire as 800 firefighters battled in vain to contain the chaos and thousands of people died of suffocation as the firestorm sucked the air out of their shelters. Some 250,000 homes were destroyed and around 1,000 factories and industrial premises, including many armaments works, which severely disrupted the enemy's war effort.

Winds of up to 250 mph and temperatures of 800 degrees Centigrade created conditions of unprecedented horror at street level and the human toll was appalling: 42,600 were killed on the ground with another 37,000 injured. There had never been such a ruinous raid upon any part of Germany before and it completely demoralised the citizens of Hamburg. One million refugees, about two-thirds of the total population, fled the city in terror and the area's industrial and logistic base was never to recover.

On the night of 29th/30th July 28 British bombers were shot down of which 26 were the victims of nightfighters. Lent claimed the only one from his *Gruppe*, a Lancaster which he intercepted on its way home off the Island of Ameland in the West Frisians. This brought his total to 73 and another promotion and another honour for him were round the next corner. On 1st August 1943 Helmut took over as *Kommodore* of a *Geschwader*, NJG 3, with his new base at Stade, west of the ruined city of Hamburg.

Typically, a *Gruppe*, which he had been commanding, consisted of three *Staffeln*, each *Staffel* having 10-12 aircraft, and the *Geschwader* consisted of three *Gruppen (see diagram of page 251)*. This meant that Helmut, at the age of 25, had over 100 nightfighters under his command. He replaced *Oberst* Hans Schalk, a Battle of Britain ace, who was 15 years older than himself. Then on 4th August a telegram from the *Führer's* Headquarters, signed by Hitler, advised him of the award of the Oak Leaves and Swords to his Knight's Cross; he was the 32nd member of the armed services to receive this honour.

On 9th he travelled again to the 'Wolf's Lair' where he was again decorated personally by Hitler and, on his return to Stade he set himself to examining entirely new nightfighter tactics now that the German radar

Schräge Musik – a mounting of two 20 mm cannon pointing upwards and forwards which enabled a nightfighter to creep up below a bomber and fire into its fuel tanks.

FROM THE OFFICIAL HANDBOOK

systems had been rendered useless by the introduction of 'Window'. However, this was never intended to give more than a temporary advantage to the RAF and the German radar operators soon learnt to recognise the hard contacts of an aircraft among the numerous and short-lived echoes received from 'Window'. In the meantime, nightfighters were experimenting with a new technique of slipping into the bomber stream and maintaining the same course and speed as the bombers until the perfect moment arrived to swoop on their prey.

Then a major breakthrough for the *Nachtjagd* came with the introduction of a new gun mounting known as *Schräge Musik*. This consisted of two 20 mm cannon mounted behind the pilot, and pointing upwards and slightly forward. It was fired by the pilot using a reflective sight after he had manoeuvred himself into position below the bomber, often without being observed. He then fired into the bomber's fuel tanks, which were located in the area between the fuselage and the inboard engines, before diving smartly out of the way before his victim exploded in a ball of fire. One of the principal advocates of the weapon, *Prinz* zu Sayn-Wittgenstein, in his stripped-down, highly-polished Junkers 88, is recorded as having shot down six Lancasters in one night. *Schräge Musik* was an extremely effective innovation and enabled the *Nachtjagd* to maintain their edge over the RAF.

Heinrich Prinz zu Sayn-Wittgenstein, an advocate of the Schräge Musik, who shot down six Lancasters in one night

Bomber Command were making advances of their own: a device known as *Serrate* which would home in on the nightfighters' radars enabled the Beaufighters and Mosquitos which were hunting them to greatly improve their results. The RAF were also introducing the system of a 'Master Bomber', a senior officer in the Pathfinder Force who would stay over the target throughout the raid guiding and encouraging all aircraft with plain language wireless transmissions and ensuring that they delivered their bombs in the right place.

August saw the start of Harris's next major offensive – the First Battle of Berlin. The night of 23rd/24th saw the first of three heavy raids with 727 aircraft but of these 56 were lost, the worst night for Bomber Command so far. The second raid on 31st August/1st September involved 622 bombers of which 47 were lost. The majority of casualties were among Stirling and Halifax aircraft with the Lancaster already beginning to prove itself as the best heavy bomber so, for the third raid on 3rd/4th September, Harris sent 316 Lancasters only, accompanied by a few Mosquitos; 22 Lancasters were lost. The results of these raids were not as satisfactory as those of the Hamburg raids and the casualties, 125 aircraft representing over 7% of the force, were not acceptable. The assault on Berlin was therefore temporarily suspended.

On 14th October the Americans learnt that unescorted daylight raids over Germany were no longer viable. A force of 251 B17s set out to destroy the ball bearing industry in Schweinfurt, a target they had previously raided in August with some success. The bombers were ruthlessly attacked by *Luftwaffe* fighters both on their way to the target and on their way back. Of the 251 bombers, 60 were shot down, a further 5 crashed in England, 12 were written off and scrapped and 121 sustained repairable damage in varying degrees. A total of 605 American airmen were killed and the Schweinfurt raid, on what became known as 'Black Thursday', is seared deep in the American consciousness.

Helmut Lent accounted for five bombers during the three Berlin raids but on the night of 2nd/3rd October he received wounds to his left hand and face while engaging a Stirling over Kassel-Harleshausen; he destroyed the bomber but his injuries grounded him until December after which he clocked up a further three kills by the end of the year bringing his total victories to 83.

The American Mustang fighter had the range to escort bombers to their European Targets.

UNITED STATES OFFICE OF WAR ADMINISTRATION 1944

The assault on Berlin resumed on 18th November and was to run for four and a half months until the end of March 1944. This was Bomber Command's most intensive operation of the war with nearly 30,000 sorties during which 1,117 bombers were lost. It also placed the greatest demands yet on the crews, many of which were just out of training and were required to undertake very long flights in freezing winter conditions which were made more hazardous than ever before by a highly organised and very experienced enemy nightfighter force. Over half the raids were on Berlin but several other cities were regularly attacked to ensure that the enemy anti-aircraft batteries were not all concentrated around the capital. As Air Marshal Harris had withdrawn the vulnerable Stirling bombers and the earlier versions of the Halifax earlier in the campaign, the battle was fought largely by Lancasters with Mosquito Pathfinders and the later versions of the Halifax.

This main Battle of Berlin can be regarded as the highpoint of the golden period of the *Nachtjagd* and culminated in the raid on Nuremberg

Junkers Ju88 which, together with the Messerschmitt bf110, was one of the main aircraft used in the nightfighter role.

BUNDESARCHIV, BILD 1011-433-0881-25A

on 30th March 1944. In a branch of the service which had become inured to appalling losses, the Nuremburg raid proved a catastrophe too far for the RAF: out of 795 aircraft 95 failed to return with 545 crewmen killed and 152 taken into captivity; it was the worst loss ever suffered by Bomber Command in a single operation. Frustrated by thick cloud over the target, the bombing had been completely ineffective with very little damage done to the city and only 69 killed on the ground.

It was, on the other hand, a field day for the *Nachtjagd* with Lent's *Geschwader* accounting for 28 kills one of which, a Halifax of 578 Squadron shot down north of the city, was his own. Since the turn of the year he had shot down 12 aircraft bringing his overall total to 94.

But across the Channel plans were well advanced for the invasion of mainland Europe and Bomber Command would be required to fill a different role in preparing the invasion coast in Normandy and, with equal endeavour, in staging raids on the French coast further north to confuse the Germans as to where the great armada was to strike. The nature of RAF bombing operations, and of the *Luftwaffe's* response would therefore change. Additionally, the appearance of the Mustang fighter, which had sufficient range to escort Allied bombers to their European targets and sufficient performance to engage and destroy the enemy interceptors, was starting to change the balance of power.

The much lauded crews of the *Nachtjagd* began to realise that the high point of their glory days was over and that from now on their victories would be harder fought.

Chapter 12 – Oak Leaves, Swords and Diamonds

The complete change of direction in the role of Bomber Command heralded an improvement of morale among crews. With the primary task of destroying road and rail links, thereby cutting off the German armies in Normandy from their sources of supply, they could see that they were now involved in what would probably be the most important operation of the war. It was also a boost for morale to know that they were now attacking military targets instead of German cities though their new role, sadly and inevitably, also caused many casualties among French civilians.

In addition to transportation, they now had an additional target in the launch sites and storage depots for Germany's new terror weapon the *V1 Vergeltungswaffe* Flying Bomb, known in Britain as the 'Doodlebug', which terrorised London and the southern counties

The V1 Flying Bomb known in Britain as the "Doodlebug"

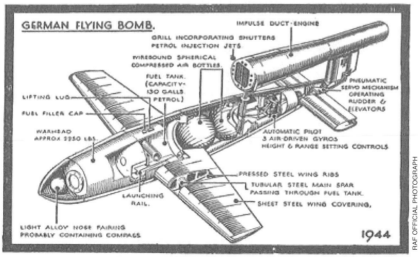

during the third quarter of 1944. The first V1 was launched against London on 13th June, one week after the Normandy Landings, and some 9,500 were despatched from then until the final sites were neutralised by advancing Allied Forces in October. The 'Doodlebug' accounted for about 23,000 civilian casualties and 800 service personnel.

Though greatly reduced in volume, there were still some old style, heavy raids on German cities. By the middle of 1944 the Americans had established themselves in 41 RAF airfields and had some 200,000 personnel in Britain who introduced a new and overwhelming level of power; they could, and on occasions did, launch a raid with 2,000 heavy bombers escorted by 1,000 fighters.

On 22nd/23rd April, 29 British aircraft out of 596 were lost in a raid on Düsseldorf which did considerable damage with over 1,000 killed on the ground. Helmut Lent destroyed one Lancaster and a further two the following month in the Osnabrück area. On 12th May he made his final operational flight in a Messerschmitt bf110, the aircraft he had flown for the past five years and in which he had made most of his kills, when he was converted to the Junkers Ju88, the other principal nightfighter used by the *Luftwaffe*.

June and July 1944 provided rich pickings for the *Nachtjagd*. The Allied Invasion in Normandy had started on 6th June and Bomber Command's main thrust was against tactical targets in France. Operating from Le Culot, an airfield at Beauvechain in central Belgium, Lent accounted for six *Viermots* during June and a further five in July. The second of these, on 21st July, was a Lancaster which he had to chase almost to the English coast before shooting it down into the sea off Deal in Kent.

On the night of 24th/25th July, the RAF mounted a series of three very heavy raids on Stuttgart over a period of five days which did immense damage and effectively destroyed the centre of the city. On the first raid 21 bombers out of 614 were lost with Lent accounting for one. On the second raid 12 out of 550 were lost and in the final raid on 28th/29th July 39 out of 496. On this night Bomber Command also sent 307 aircraft to Hamburg of which 22 were lost

Cockpit of a Junkers Ju88 as flown by Lent from May 1944.

and two of which were destroyed by Lent bringing his overall total
to 108. Two days later he was awarded the Oak Leaves with Swords
and Diamonds to his Knight's Cross of the Iron Cross, popularly
known as the *Brillanten*, the highest award that could be made to
German servicemen at the time. *Reichsmarschall* Hermann Göring,
Commander-in-Chief of the Luftwaffe, wrote to congratulate him:

> "Full of pride and gratitude I congratulate you on the
> highest German decoration for gallantry which you,
> the first and most successful German nightfighter,
> now wear. No one is more able than I am to measure
> what unforgettable services you have performed in
> the battle for the destiny of the German people
>   "With unbridled readiness for action and death-
> defying bravery, you have fought night after night to

defend our homeland against the enemy's terror bombers, destroying opponent after opponent. It is your example which invariably motivates the men of your *Geschwader* to gallant feats of arms in the most bitter conflicts. In you, therefore, the entire German nation joins me in our admiration of one of our bravest soldiers. I combine my acknowledgement of your glorious achievements, both as a single combatant and a commanding officer, with my best wishes for your future and further proud victories."

On 24th August, one week after shooting down his 109th bomber following a raid on Kiel, Lent returned to the 'Wolf's Lair' at Rastenburg to receive his *Brillanten* from the *Führer*. This was the apex of his recognition and his glory. From Rastenburg he returned to his old base at Stade and on the 12th and 17th of September won his 110th and 111th victories.

Helmut had promised his friend, *Oberstleutnant* Hans-Joachim Jabs, who was commanding NJG1, that he would visit him for a discussion on operational techniques and early in October 1944 a suitable opportunity arose. He took off from Stade at 1246 on Thursday 5th for the flight to Paderborn where Jabs was stationed. He was flying his regular aircraft, a Junkers 88, and as well as his trusty *Funker*, Walter Kubisch, he was carrying two passengers, ostensibly as members of his crew – *Leutnant* Werner Kark, a war correspondent listed as a gunner, and *Oberleutnant* Hermann Klöss as Second *Funker* under Kubisch.

It was a fine day for the one-and-a-half hour, 140-mile flight and he

Oak Leaves with Swords and Diamonds, the ultimate addition to the Knight's Cross of the Iron Cross, popularly known as the "Brillanten".

GNU FREE DOCUMENTATION LICENCE

Lent with Walter Kubisch his crewman and friend who flew with him for most of his service.

arrived at Paderborn-Nordborchen airfield at 1320 shortly after the departure of a force of American bombers which had raided the airfield and left several craters in the runway. An emergency grass runway had been marked out for Lent's landing; there was an electric power cable on the approach run but this had not been considered a potential hazard.

There were several eyewitnesses to what happened next, all of whose accounts varied slightly in detail though they essentially told the same story. Lent's aircraft had come in with its port engine stopped and its undercarriage retracted. The ground controller had fired two red flares to warn him. Lent started a tight turn to port, possibly because he had seen the overhead cable, the aircraft stalled and the port wing hit the ground while the starboard wing cut through the electric cable. There was a bright blue flash and the aircraft burst into flames as it crashed to the ground.

Surprisingly, all four of the crew were thrown out of the crash and members of the ground staff rushed to the scene to drag the victims clear and await arrival of the emergency ambulances. They were taken to the Paderborn Hospital but all four were unconscious

Lent wearing his "Brillanten" shortly before his fatal accident.

and very severely injured. Walter Kubisch whose body had suffered multiple fractures, died on the operating table shortly after arrival as surgeons struggled to stem his horrific injuries. Klöss died later in the day and Kark the following morning both with grievous head wounds.

Helmut had compound fractures in both lower legs and was suffering from concussion though he had received the least serious injuries of the four. Amputation of one leg was proposed as there was a risk of gangrene but *Reichsmarschall* Göring intervened insisting that the operation should wait until Professor Häberle, a senior *Luftwaffe* surgeon, had taken charge of the case. Häberle considered that the shock of amputation would kill the patient and undertook a very skillful pinning of the fractures instead.

Helmut regained consciousness after this operation to find his old friend Hans-Joachim Jabs at his bedside with news that Lena had given birth to another daughter, Helma. He was very disappointed that it was not a son. He also told Jabs that he had no memory of the crash and could not account for what had caused it. The next day, Saturday 7th October, it was found that despite their precautions gangrene had set in and there was no alternative to amputation. Helmut was too weak to survive the shock and died on the operating table.

Helmut Lent was such a well-known and revered national figure that much discussion and speculation took place after his death both on the cause of the crash and of his subsequent death. There is still no certainty of exactly what happened as the Ju88 came in to land. An examination of the port engine revealed that there was a fault which would have stopped it but nobody knew at what stage it had been shut down or had stopped of its own accord. The propeller had been feathered which would have been standard procedure to reduce drag, and the undercarriage was retracted suggesting that either Lent intended to make a belly landing or, which is generally considered more probable, he was having a look at the ground before going round again. This latter is supported by the fact that the aircraft's flaps were not in the landing position.

The reason for his sudden turn to port is similarly inconclusive: it may have been because he spotted the overhead cable at the last moment or possibly because he was distracted by the red flares fired from the ground to warn him about his undercarriage.

Another theory is that, in an effort to climb away to go round again, he opened the throttle of the starboard engine too violently which caused the aircraft to spin round on its port wing. Helmut was an extremely experienced and skillful pilot but, in the absence of conclusive evidence, the official verdict was pilot error.

As far as his death is concerned, it is known that the senior doctor at the Paderborn Hospital ordered an immediate amputation which might have averted any chance of gangrene setting in. It is thought that the delay caused by Göring's intervention and insistence on, in effect, a second opinion, may have sealed his fate but, on the other hand, Professor Häberle's view that the patient could not have withstood the shock of amputation at that stage may have been correct; in which case death was inevitable either way.

Helmut was posthumously promoted to *Oberst* and his crewman and friend, Walter Kubisch, was commissioned in the rank of *Leutnant*. On 11th October 1944 a Service of Remembrance was

Luftwaffe Commander-in-Chief, Hermann Göring, speaking at the Service of Remembrance for Oberst Helmut Lent in the Reichchancellery, Berlin, 11th October 1944.

held in the Reichchancellery in Berlin with Lent's coffin being carried by six officers, all holders of The Knight's Cross. Leading the cortege was *Oberstleutnant* Werner Streib, the Inspector of Nightfighters, holding Lent's medals and decorations on a velvet cushion.

Reichsmarschall Göring took the salute as the coffin entered the Reichchancellery and then gave an impassioned address which included the following tribute to a great German and gallant officer:

> " . . . A man who achieves so many things, such a warrior, such an example and such a teacher, will forever live with us and among us. Just as he was the model for the new force, so too will his spirit mark the *Nachtjagd* in the future. As we take our leave from him at this hour, and as we remember his life, we cannot but be aware that his sacrifice imposes a duty on us all, the duty to be worthy of that sacrifice. The life of a hero such as this cannot be snuffed out and, at this very moment when the battle to the end will be most difficult, we too feel the strength to fight it.
>
> "At this hour of farewell, my dear Lent, the *Führer* expresses his recognition and thanks to you to which I add those of the *Luftwaffe*, the gratitude of the German people and my personal thanks. Today when dark clouds surround Germany, the deeds of men such as you will shine so brightly that we need not fear the darkness. You were ready to fight and to die and now, my good and gallant Lent, join the ranks of the heroes."

The following day Lent's body was moved to the *Luftwaffe* base at Stade, his final operational base, where it was buried in the military cemetery together with the bodies of his three crew members.

Chapter 13 – Aftermath

In 1945, though she had had three years to come to terms with Alec's loss, Nessie would still not accept that he was dead and still harboured the hope that he was a prisoner-of-war or hiding out in some brave and friendly community in Holland. Being one of many thousands of RAF parents/wives/widows frantically trying to obtain details of the loss of their loved ones, she made little progress with the Air Ministry who could only send out standard replies assuring relatives that everything possible was being done to account for every missing airman. She wrote to the Ministry again on 24th July suggesting that Alec might have lost his memory and be wandering around Europe. They replied on 9th August:

> **"I am directed to refer to your letter of 24th July, 1945, and to express the Departments'** *(sic)* **regret at the delay in replying thereto, owing to the great increase in casualty enquiries consequent upon the occupation of enemy territory.**
>
> **"Unhappily, no further news has been received in this Department regarding your husband or any member of the crew, apart from that which has already been conveyed to you in previous correspondence.**
>
> **"I am to explain that the names of all personnel who have been prisoners, or in hiding, are now known, and immediately prisoners of war are liberated, their particulars are taken and their next of kin informed by telegram. It is deeply regretted that your husband's name was not among these.**
>
> **"I am further to explain that there are no known cases of Royal Air Force personnel suffering from loss of memory either at home or overseas.**
>
> **"In view of these circumstances, and of the fact that no news has been received since the date he was presumed to have lost his life, apart from the recovery of**

the body of one member of the crew from the sea at Heligoland, we are faced with the sad conclusion that your husband's aircraft came down in the sea, and that her crew was lost with her.

"In conveying this sad conclusion, I am to express the Department's sympathy with you in your great loss you have susta*(ined)***"**

Nessie was still not satisfied that every stone had been turned. The Press at the time was full of rumours, all of which were spurious, of servicemen who had lost their memories and were wandering around former-occupied Europe. She therefore solicited the aid of her father, Andrew Gilzean, who was Member of Parliament for Edinburgh Central, in the hope that his position, and the fact that he spent much of his time at the House of Commons in London, might enable him to obtain more information than she could herself.

Gilzean called at the Casualty Branch of the Air Ministry in Oxford Street and put his daughter's hopes and fears before Group Captain, R. Burges, who explained with sympathy, and in great detail, the reasons why any hopes of finding Alec alive were effectively nil. Gilzean asked if he could confirm what he had told him in writing lest any point should slip his memory when relaying their conversation to Nessie. The Group Captain wrote:

"You were kind enough to call here and discuss the position regarding your son-in-law, Pilot Officer A.J.S. Ollar D.F.M., who was reported missing in July 1942, and you asked me to write more fully regarding certain points of your enquiry in order to satisfy the questions which continue to disturb Mrs. Ollar. It gives me great pleasure to do so, and I shall be very glad if a statement of the facts as we have them should go towards resolving the doubts which your daughter so reasonably feels.

"It is true that our records show nothing further about Pilot Officer Ollar or his crew than that the body of Pilot Officer Whittaker was recovered from the sea and

The Missing Research and Enquiry Service has been operating in a small way all this year, and has been able to resolve already a large number of family uncertainties. I can inform you, in confidence, that the Service is in process of being developed on a considerably larger scale with the intention of making a thorough search all over Europe so far as geographical and political conditions allow.

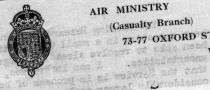

TELEPHONE: GERRARD 9234
Extn.................

ANY communications on the subject of this letter should be addressed to :—
THE
UNDER SECRETARY
OF STATE
and the following number quoted :—
Your Ref. .... P.371508/42/P.4.Cas.

AIR MINISTRY
(Casualty Branch)
73-77 OXFORD STREET
W.1

22 August, 1945.

Dear Sir,

You were kind enough to call here and discuss the position regarding your son-in-law, Pilot Officer A.J.S. Ollar, D.F.M., who was reported missing in July 1942, and you asked me to write more fully regarding certain points of your enquiry in order to satisfy the questions which continue to disturb Mrs. Ollar. It gives me great pleasure to do so, and I shall be very glad indeed if a statement of the facts as we have them should go towards resolving the doubts which your daughter so reasonably feels.

It is true that our records show nothing further about Pilot Officer Ollar or his crew than that the body of Pilot Officer Whittaker was recovered from the sea and buried at Oberland, Heligoland. Unfortunately, a good deal of misleading matter on the subject of the missing and the problem of looking for them has appeared in the press, but it is true, of course, that there are a very large number of men of whom we have to find traces: I should make it clear, however, that the R.A.F. Missing Research and Enquiry Service to which your daughter refers is established for the purpose only of obtaining traces and endeavouring to make certain the fate of the missing; we do not expect to find missing personnel alive, though we should be only too grateful if we were able to do so.

/The

Andrew Gilzean, Esq., M.P.,
House of Commons,
S.W.1.

W. Burges.

(Group Captain in Casualty Branch)

buried at Oberland, Heligoland. Unfortunately, a good deal of misleading matter on the subject of the missing and the problem of looking for them has appeared in the press, but it is true, of course, that there are a very large number of men of whom we have to find traces: I should make it clear, however, that the R.A.F. Missing Research and Enquiry Service to which your daughter refers is established for the purpose only of obtaining traces and endeavouring to make certain the fate of the missing; we do not expect to find missing personnel alive, though we should be only too grateful if we were able to do so.

"The Missing Research and Enquiry Service has been operating in a small way all this year, and has been able to resolve already a large number of family uncertainties. I can inform you, in confidence, that the Service is in process of being developed on a considerably larger scale with the intention of making a thorough search all over Europe so far as geographical and political conditions allow.

"It is impossible to accord any special priority to any casualty enquiry; the Frisian Islands, those off the coast of Denmark and Heligoland will be searched, and the authorities and as many of the inhabitants as possible questioned regarding any traces or knowledge they may have of aircrew, but in view of the magnitude of the task before us it is quite impossible to promise results by any definite date.

"Regarding loss of memory, I am afraid that a great many unhappy and groundless rumours have been spread. I have no note of any case of loss of memory in the Air Force, and the Medical Authorities assure me that they have no records of any. We have not a photograph of your son-in-law, but our experience of endeavouring to identify people from photographs is negative. It is found, on the one hand, that a past photograph rarely compares sufficiently with the original, and on the other hand when unnamed photographs have been published, the claimants to them have numbered in some cases upwards of a hundred.

"It is not that we are hopeless of good news. There is always, except where death is definitely proved, the millionth chance, but I am bound to add that experience of many thousands of cases which we have had in this war leads us to the unfortunate conclusion that the chances of Pilot Officer Ollar being alive are too remote for serious consideration.

"It is probable that a number of unidentified graves will be found, either by ourselves or by the Army Graves Service, with whom we have a very close liaison, around the coast, as your daughter suggests, and it may be possible in some cases to identify their occupants. In the latter case, we should inform the next-of-kin concerned, but it has never been the policy of the Air Ministry to act on suspicion only, and we certainly do not impart information without what we regard as reasonable proof.

"I hope that I have now been able to give you reasonable replies to some of the points which you raised, and I can only conclude by assuring you again of the intention of the Air Ministry to take all possible steps to trace those who are missing. It is indeed unfortunate that so many misleading rumours are current in the press and otherwise, but we feel satisfied that by now all those, both prisoners-of-war and others, who are capable of returning and wish to do so have already come back.

"May I ask you to express my sympathy and that of the whole Casualty Branch with your daughter in this very long period of anxiety which she is experiencing."

Eight years later, on 17th October 1953, Nessie together with Alec's sister Mary and her son, attended the unveiling by Her Majesty The Queen of the Runnymede Memorial, on the fields where the Magna Carta was signed.

The Runnymede Air Forces Memorial.

This impressive edifice records the names of 20,456 personnel of the British and Commonwealth Air Forces who were lost without trace and have no known grave. Alec's name is there alongside those of many hundreds of airmen with whom he served.

His name was also included on the War Memorial in Campbeltown, where he spent most of his childhood, and also, together with two others, on a Memorial Plaque in the offices of the North British and Mercantile Insurance Company at 64 Princes Street, Edinburgh. The company, now a

Alec's name on the Runnymede Memorial commemorating 20,456 airmen who were lost in World War II and have no known grave.

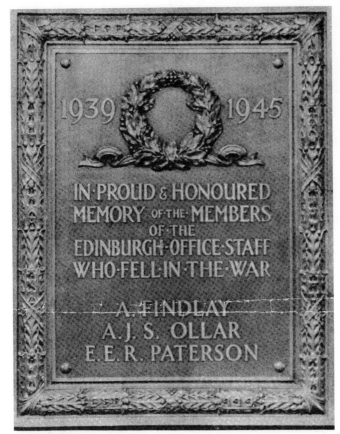

Memorial plaque erected at the offices of the North British and Mercantile Insurance Company in their head-quarters at 64 Princes Street, Edinburgh. The building is now a branch of Britsh Home Stores and the plaque has disappeared

part of Aviva, sold its premises in 1960 and the building is now a branch of British Home Stores. The plaque has sadly disappeared without trace.

Alec's best friend, Murray Collins, served through the war in the Royal Artillery during which he was wounded and finished his army service in command of a Prisoner-of-War camp in the Far East. When he was released from the army he returned to his old job at the North British and Mercantile Insurance Company where he served for many years and became a senior manager before accepting a post in local government. In the late 1950s, having, rather charmingly, sought and obtained the prior blessing of Alec's family, Nessie married Murray Collins. Murray was an enthusiastic yachtsman and the couple sailed his boat in the Forth racing events as well as cruising to Europe and the Mediterranean. They lived happily in Edinburgh until Nessie died in 1998. Murray died in 2007 aged 97.

On 1st January 1943 an RAF station at Davidstow Moor, Cornwall, became operational and was host to a number of different squadrons, with different roles and flying different aircraft, until the station's closure in 1945. Mrs Stock, proprietor of the Wellington Hotel in nearby Boscastle, whose son Johnny had been lost in the same aircraft as Alec, took the station personnel into her heart and home and the saloon bar of the hotel became, almost, an extension of the officers' mess on the station. To many youngsters far from home she became a mother figure and the front door key was left under the mat so no officer would ever be denied access. For three months in 1944, 524 Squadron was at Davidstow Moor and when they moved to Norfolk they presented her with a token of the affection in which she was held – a silver tray inscribed with the signatures of the Commanding Officer, Squadron Leader A W R Naismith and other officers of the squadron.

A silver tray presentrd to Mrs A Stock, owner of the Wellington Hotel in nearby Boscastle, by officers of 524 Squadron stationed at RAF Davidstow Moor, Cornwall

ROD & ANNE KNIGHT

The Canadian member of Alec's crew, Flight Sergeant William Kostyshyn, was commemorated by the people of Melville, Saskatchewan, in a different way. A framed photograph of him hangs on the wall of the town hospital but, even more lastingly, it was decided to call a lake after him to honour a son of Melville who answered his country's call to arms. Kostyshyn Lake, 93 kilometres from the town of McLennan Lake in the wild and beautiful uplands of Saskatchewan, serves as a permanent memorial to a local man who gave his life in the cause of freedom.

Kostyshyn Lake
Named in Memory of
William Martin Kostyshyn
Melville, Saskatchewan
Royal Canadian Air Force
Flight Sergeant, R75325
On Active Service To His Country
Missing in Action
July 27, 1942
Age 22
Commemorative Inscription
Runnymede War Memorial
Surrey, England

ED KOSTYSHYN

In March 1944 Wing Commander Alan Cousens DSO, DFC, after a posting to Headquarters Bomber Command and a course at the RAF Staff College, was chosen by Air Vice Marshal Bennet to command the newly-formed 635 Pathfinder Squadron flying Lancasters from RAF Downham Market in Norfolk.

The following month on 22nd April 1944 a large scale attack was launched on the railway yards at Laon by 181 aircraft of Bomber Command. Among them was Lancaster ND508 commanded by Alan Cousens who was a designated Master Bomber in the operation. The attack was conducted in two waves and obtained excellent results with considerable damage to the railway yards but having left the target and set a course for home, ND508 was shot down and Wing Commander Cousens and six other crew members were killed. The pilot, Pilot Officer D H Courtency, was the only one to survive and was later captured. Alan Cousens, together with the other crew members, is buried in Roye New British Cemetery in France.

Alan's widow, Nan, married again after the war and together with Alan's son, Michael, emigrated to the Argentine. His descendants are now Spanish speaking Argentine citizens.

Most of the aircrew with whom Alec flew during his service were not to survive the war. As previously recorded, Cyril Wessels was shot down by *Hauptmann* Werner Streib in October 1940 and Philip Forrester and Thomas Woor were killed in the same aircraft in Malta in November 1940. Archie Roberts, Alec's close friend since gunnery training days was killed in January 1941 when his Wellington crashed at Great Wratting, Suffolk, during an air test. Sergeant Pilot John Molony did not live to inherit his baronetcy and was lost in March 1941; Flight Lieutenant Charles Petley was killed the following July and Pilot Officer John Berry in November.

Squadron Leader Norman Mulholland, the Australian pilot who had difficulty in understanding the Scots members of his crew, was lost in February 1942 while serving with 458 (RAAF) Squadron and Flight Lieutenant John Sword in May. Another Australian, Flight Sergeant Robert Stoddart, was killed three months after Alec in October during operations at El Alamein. Norman Stent, the pilot who earned Alec's praise for his meticulous target location, was killed in an accident in February 1943 while flying a Lancaster of 100 Squadron; he was aged 23 and had reached the rank of Flight Lieutenant. Yet another Australian, wireless operator Sergeant George Cleverly, who flew with Alec during his first tour, was killed during a raid on Hanover in October 1943.

Of the special crew who delivered Queen Wilhelmina's birthday gift to the Dutch people in August 1941, not one survived the war. Flight Sergeant Wilfred Wooldridge was posted to the Far East and was killed four months later in December 1941. Squadron Leader Martin Stephens DFC, Air Gunner and former Shooting Editor of *The Field*, was shot down in February 1942 and is buried at Flushing on the Dutch Island of Walcheren. The New Zealand pilot, Squadron Leader Thomas McGillivray DFC, was lost in May 1942 over the Ardennes and Percy 'Pick' Pickard, having reached the rank of Group Captain at the age of 28 with a DSO and two bars and a DFC, was shot down in February 1944 in his Mosquito by an Fw190 German fighter during 'Operation Jericho' – the daring low-level attack on Amiens Prison in an attempt to free members of the French Resistance imprisoned there.

The youngest 115 Squadron pilot who took part in Alec's last operation was 18 year-old Walter Norrington from Hove in Sussex. He survived until March 1945 when he was killed in the battle for Enfidaville in Tunisia. He was a Flight Sergeant and 21 years of age. Another youngster who flew on some of the same operations as Alec, Ivor Slade, was killed on 24th August 1943; he was a Flight Lieutenant, aged 19 with a DFC.

Sergeant Glafkos Cleredes, Sergeant Fereday's wireless operator who had baled out over Germany believing the rest of the crew to have already done so, survived the war in a German Prisoner-of-War Camp and after his repatriation studied for and obtained a law degree in London. Returning to his native Cyprus he then became a member of EOKA the terrorist organisation dedicated to ending

CYPRUS MAIL

Wireless Operator Sergeant Glafkos Cleredes who became the fourth President of Cyprus.

BRIEF SQUADRON HISTORY
115 SQUADRON
(FROM THE BOMBER COMMAND WAR DIARIES)

SERVICE

IN 3 GROUP FROM THE OUTBREAK UNTIL THE END OF THE WAR. FLEW WELLINGTONS AND LANCASTERS FROM MARHAM, MILDENHALL, EAST WRETHAM, LITTLE SNORING AND WITCHFORD.
DETACHED TO COASTAL COMMAND FOR ONE SHORT PERIOD IN APRIL 1940.

OPERATIONAL PERFORMANCE

RAIDS FLOWN

WELLINGTONS – 332 BOMBING, 54 MINELAYING, 4 LEAFLET
LANCASTERS – 261 BOMBING, 27 MINELAYING
TOTAL – 593 BOMBING, 81 MINELAYING, 4 LEAFLET = 678 RAIDS

SORTIES AND LOSSES

WELLINGTONS – 3,075 SORTIES, 98 AIRCRAFT LOST (3.2 PER CENT)
LANCASTERS – 4,678 SORTIES, 110 AIRCRAFT LOST (2.4 PER CENT)
TOTAL – 7,753 SORTIES, 208 AIRCRAFT LOST (2.7 PER CENT)
22 LANCASTERS WERE DESTROYED IN CRASHES.

POINTS OF INTEREST

115 SQUADRON HAD ONE OF THE FINEST RECORDS OF OPERATIONAL SERVICE IN BOMBER COMMAND.

AN ORIGINAL SQUADRON ON THE OUTBREAK OF WAR AND, EXCEPT FOR ONE VERY SHORT PERIOD OF DETACHMENT TO COASTAL COMMAND, SERVED CONTINUOUSLY UNTIL THE END OF THE WAR.

CARRIED OUT THE FIRST GEE TRIALS IN AUGUST 1941.

CARRIED OUT THE THIRD HIGHEST NUMBER OF BOMBING RAIDS IN BOMBER COMMAND HEAVY SQUADRONS AND THE MOST RAIDS IN 3 GROUP.

FLEW THE SECOND HIGHEST NUMBER OF SORTIES IN BOMBER COMMAND.

PROBABLY DROPPED THE SECOND GREATEST TONNAGE OF BOMBS, APPROXIMATELY 23,000 TONS, IN BOMBER COMMAND. DROPPED MORE BOMBS THAN ANY OTHER SQUADRON IN 3 GROUP.

SUFFERED THE MOST LOSSES IN THE WHOLE OF BOMBER COMMAND: THE ONLY SQUADRON TO LOSE MORE THAN 200 AIRCRAFT IN THE WAR.

CARRIED OUT MOST RAIDS, FLEW MOST SORTIES AND SUFFERED MOST LOSSES OF ANY WELLINGTON SQUADRON IN BOMBER COMMAND.

CARRIED OUT MOST RAIDS, FLEW MOST SORTIES, SUFFERED MOST LOSSES AND THE HIGHEST PERCENTAGE LOSS RATE IN ANY LANCASTER SQUADRON IN 3 GROUP.

DR A PILLING

115 Squadron – 'One of the finest records of operational service in Bomber Command.' Plaque on the Squadron Memorial.

British rule and responsible for the murder of over 100 British servicemen in the 1950s. After a distinguished legal career including the defence of EOKA terrorists and investigation of alleged British human rights abuses, Cleredes became the fourth President of Cyprus from 1993 to 2003. He died in November 2013.

The 115 Squadron Memorial which is situated just inside the entrance to the Lancaster Way Business Park on the site of the former RAF Witchford near Ely, Cambridgeshire.

DR A PILLING

Little remains today of the airfields and establishments where Alec served. RAF Grangemouth is now an industrial area and the great intake establishment at RAF Padgate is now covered by a housing estate. RAF Evanton where Alec attended the Air Gunnery School was closed in 1947 and is now an industrial estate. Newmarket is no longer an RAF station but has a grass strip for the use of light aircraft. RAF Harwell is today the Atomic Energy Research Establishment and RAF Stradishall, where Alec did his gunnery instructors' course, is now the site of two category 'C' prisons.

PATHE NEWS

Then and now. The spot in front of the hangars at RAF Marham
where aircrews gathered after the first raid on Berlin in 1940,
and the same spot today.

SQUADRON LEADER A RICHARDSON

RAF Marham, however, from where Alec flew on both his operational tours, is today an extremely active and important frontline station operating (in 2015) three squadrons of GR4/GR4a Tornadoes and preparing to receive the RAFs Lightning Force in the near future. With its huge support infrastructure, the station employs around 10,000 people. Having made a very great contribution to victory in World War 2, the station today continues to play a vital role in support of present-day conflicts.

In 1943 115 Squadron, now equipped with Lancasters, moved from Marham to RAF Witchford near Ely in Cambridgeshire. The Squadron Memorial is located on the site of the old airfield, which is today an industrial estate. Close by is a small collection of memorabilia of the wartime station displayed by courtesy of a local firm on their premises.

The massive contribution to victory made by the Americans is not forgotten with several US aircraft and buildings preserved at some of the former USAAF airfields. One such is at Thorpe Abbotts former RAF station near Diss in Norfolk which houses the 100th Bomb Group Memorial Museum containing an excellent collection of memorabilia of Britain's great and gallant ally. The US 8th Air Force in England lost some 26,000 men killed in action during World War 2, nearly half of those killed in RAF Bomber Command. Thorpe Abbotts is run by volunteers who have also restored the control tower

Despite the fact that over 11,000 Wellington Bombers were built, and that it bore the brunt of the bomber offensive in the early years of the war, and was the only marque to be in front-line service throughout the whole war, only two examples of this famous aircraft still exist – neither in airworthy condition. One is the property of the RAF Museum and is at present (2015) under restoration at their Cosford premises. The second is an aircraft which crashed in Loch Ness in 1940 and was raised in 1985 and restored over a number of years. It is now on show at the Brooklands Museum in Surrey. Looking at the cramped space in the rear gun turret it is difficult to imagine how those stalwart air gunners could sit in there for seven or eight hours, cold, uncomfortable and isolated from the rest of their crew, and remain alert and vigilant.

* * *

DR A PILLING

Of the 11,000 Vickers Wellington Bombers built, only two examples survive:

Above: An aircraft which crashed into Loch Ness in 1940, was raised in 1985 and, after several years of restoration, was placed on display at the Brooklands Museum in Surrey where it may be seen today.

Below: An aircraft belonging to the RAF Museum which is currently undergoing restoration at Cosford.

PLANE-CRAZY-HOSTING.CO.UK

After Helmut Lent's death, his family were, once again, to come into conflict with the *Nazi* establishment. Following publication of an obituary notice in the German national press, proceedings were started by the *Gestapo* against his widow Lena, his father Pastor Johannes Lent, and the editor of the newspaper concerned because, though acknowledging Helmut's Christian beliefs, the notice made no reference to the *Führer* and was therefore deemed to be 'anti-*Nazi*'. His family were saved from being sent to a concentration camp as they were able to prove that the obituary had been written in advance by Helmut himself specifically omitting any reference to the *Führer* or the *Nazi* state.

But the family's troubles were far from over: the village of Pyrehne was in the direct path of the Russian advance on Berlin and when the Red Army arrived the church was blown up to make way for an advanced airfield. The villagers were used as slave labour, houses were looted and women raped. On 16th February 1945, Pastor Lent was shot by a drunken Russian soldier in the doorway of his own house and his wife and daughter Ursula turned out on the street. Like thousands of other displaced persons in Europe, they wandered around, hiding Ursula from the Russian soldiers in haylofts and cellars until they eventually settled in Bülzig in East Germany. Helmut's widow Lena and their two daughters were more fortunate as they finished the war in the Allied sector of Germany.

With the realignment of European boundaries after the war, the village of Pyrehne, where Helmut Lent was born, is now in Poland rather than Germany and no trace remains of the family's home or church.

Many *Nachtjagd* aces did not survive the war although their rate of attrition was less than that of the bomber crewmen they fought. Among Lent's fellow warriors *Oberstleutnant* Paul Gildner [48 victories] was killed in 1943 and *Hauptmann* Manfred Meurer [65] and *Hauptmann* Heinz Strünning [56] in 1944. *Major Prinz* Heinrich zu Sayn-Wittgenstein [83 including six Lancasters in one night] was killed in 1944; the other nightfighter prince, *Major Prinz* Egmont zur Lippe-Weissenfeld was killed in a flying accident in the same year.

The only *Nachtjagd* pilot who exceeded Helmut Lent's score of 110 was *Major* Heinz-Wolfgang Schnaufer, known to British bomber crews

The Australian crew of a Halifax of 462 squadron in 1945. They are standing beside the Messerschmitt bf110 of Major Heinz-Wolfgang Schnaufer, 'The Spook of Saint Trond' who accounted for 121 Allied aircraft. The tail fin of his aircraft carries a symbol for each of his victories and is preserved today in the Australian War Memorials Collection.

as 'The Spook of Saint Trond', who destroyed a total of 121 aircraft including nine Lancasters on the night of 21st February 1945, the last seven of which were shot down within a period of 19 minutes. Like Lent, he was awarded the coveted *Brillanten*, the Knight's Cross of the Iron Cross with Oak Leaves, Swords and Diamonds. After the war Schnaufer ran his family's wine business and was killed in 1948, aged 28, in a road traffic accident in France when his Mercedes collided with a lorry.

Others who survived the war included *Major* Rudolf Schoenert [64] who died in 1985, *Oberstleutnant* Werner Streib [68 including Cyril Wessels] in the following year, *Oberstleutnant* Gunter Radüsch [65] in 1988 and *Major* Paul Zorner [58] who died in 2014 aged 94. Lent's great friend, *Oberstleutnant* Hans Joachim Jabs [50] died in 2003 and *Leutnant* Leopold Fellerer, 'The Viermot Specialist', having joined the Austrian airforce after the war, was killed in a flying accident in 1968.

Examples of both the great German nightfighters, the Messer-schmitt bf110 and the Junkers Ju88 are preserved and on display at the RAF Museum in Hendon. Of the principal airfields in Holland from which Helmut Lent operated, Lieuwarden is an operational Royal Dutch Air Force station and Deelen is still in occasional use. However, many of the old Luftwaffe buildings can still be seen around the Deelen airfield and one such houses an excellent small museum which has been built up and is run by dedicated and enthusiastic volunteers. Many exhibits are remains and equipment from crashed aircraft where the circumstances of the crash, the personnel involved and often their descendants have been researched and chronicled for the interest of visitors.

The Museum at the former Luftwaffe Nightfighter Airfield at Deelen. DR A PILLING

Examples of the two great Luftwaffe nightfighters on display at the
RAF Museum , Hendon – the Messerschmitt bf110 *(above)* and the
Junkers Ju88 *(below)*. The Junkers came into British possession
when its crew defected to the UK in 1943.

Motorcycles at the 'Deelen Dump'.

Deelen Airfield is also the site of the 'Deelen Dump' where, after the war, the Canadians left around 37,000 vehicles – tanks, scout cars, lorries, jeeps and motorcycles – as it was cheaper to abandon them than to ship them back to Canada. These vehicles formed the first step in a restored civil transport network in Holland where all private and commercial vehicles had been requisitioned or destroyed during the German occupation.

The change of management at Deelen is recorded poignantly in a small spinney near the former *Luftwaffe* officers' mess where a tree is carved with a swastika and the year 1941; beside it is a tree carved with 'Canada' and the date 1945.

❧

Luftwaffe relics at Deelen.

Above: **Barrack block.**

Below: **Officers' Mess.**

Right: **One of several farmhouses around the perimeter of the airfield built as nightfighter dispersal hangars but disguised as farmhouses.**

Epilogue

'Reaping the Whirlwind'

After the war, politicians who had enthusiastically supported the activities of Bomber Command when Britain was in danger of being overwhelmed by the Nazis, and media personnel who had given sparse coverage to the few voices of dissension at the time, suddenly developed consciences and began to question the morality of area bombing. Before World War I there was no such thing as aerial bombardment and, to form any sort of informed judgement on the moral and strategic aspects of area bombing it is necessary to examine its origins, development and implementation.

The First World War had been the catalyst needed by the infant aircraft industry to give top priority to research and development and there can be no doubt that, without the war, the industry in 1918 would have been several years behind what it actually was. During this period, therefore, there were enormous advances in aircraft design and openings for far greater scope in their military deployment. The first aerial raids on civilian targets were undertaken in January 1915 by the German Navy, widely condemned in Britain as 'The Baby Killers', using airships which would become known collectively as *Zeppelins*. In the course of the war some 50 *Zeppelin* raids were mounted upon Britain killing 557 civilians and injuring 1,358. Raids were also made on civilian targets in Belgium and France, the historic cathedral of Notre Dame being damaged in one of the regular raids on Paris.

"GOD PUNISHES ENGLAND"

A German postage stamp depicting a Zeppelin machine-gunning a ground target in Britain.

WWW.PHILATELETICDATABASE.COM

From 1917 the *Zeppelins*, though still active, started to be augmented with the more effective *Gotha G.V* long-range, heavy bomber. The first raid was on 25th May 1917 when 23 *Gothas* set out to bomb London but because of cloud cover over the capital, attacked Folkestone instead killing 95 and injuring 195. Bombing of British towns and cities continued throughout the war; the last *Gotha* raid on Britain was in May 1918 and the last *Zeppelin* raid later in the year in August. Over a period of three and a half years these missions, ranging from Kent to the Firth of Forth, had killed 1,413 British civilians and injured 4,822.

A German Gotha long-range heavy bomber of the type which regularly claimed civilian casualties in Britain during 1917/18. It was powered by two Mercedes engines and had a range of 522 miles.

There had been no coyness or ambiguity about the purpose of these raids; the policy had the blessing of the *Kaiser* and had been summarised by Grand Admiral von Tirpitz, head of the German Navy, in a statement which confirmed Germany's view on the legitimacy of area bombing to break civilian morale:

> **" The measure of the success will be not only in the injury which will be caused to the enemy, but also the significant effect it will have in diminishing the enemy's determination to prosecute the war."**

Following the Gotha raids of 1917, the inevitability of strategic bombing began to be recognised. On 1st April 1918 the Royal Air Force was inaugurated by the amalgamation of the Royal Naval Air Service and the

Royal Flying Corps and the following month the Independent Air Force, also known as the Independent Bombing Force, was formed with the express purpose of attacking German industrial targets, airfields and railways. For the remaining five months of the war the Independent Force dropped 550 tons of bombs on targets in Germany with the loss of 109 aircraft thereby giving forewarning of the heavy casualty rates which could be expected in future bombing operations. Just before the end of the war the British bomber squadrons were joined by French, Italian and US squadrons to form the Inter-Allied Independent Air Force, the first Allied strategic bombing force. This was disbanded at the end of hostilities but not before the leaders of the national contingents – Marshal of the RAF Trenchard, General Mitchell of the USAAF and General Douhet of the Italian Air Force – had recognised that strategic bombing was here to stay and that victory in future wars would depend largely on area bombing to destroy the enemy's industry and break civilian morale.

With ever advancing ordnance technology and bigger and better aircraft, it was evident that civilian casualties would be frighteningly heavy and several attempts were made during the 1920s and 30s to introduce some form of control on aerial bombardment and even, in one instance, to ban it altogether. However, diverse national interests and the practical difficulties of regulation frustrated any sort of agreement. By the time war came again in 1939 no accord had been achieved other than a general feeling that the killing of women and children in war was undesirable, and should be avoided wherever possible, but would, on occasions, be inevitable in the conduct of modern warfare.

At the outset of the Second World War, Britain and France acceded to a plea from the neutral United States that aerial bombing should be restricted to military targets, but they acceded on the understanding that all belligerent nations should exercise the same restraint. However, at dawn on 1st September 1939 the *Luftwaffe* commenced the invasion of Poland with the destruction of the city of Nieluń which killed 1,200 civilians. This was the first of many attacks on civilian targets in Poland including the huge columns of refugees which blocked the roads as they fled from their destroyed towns and cities. Although the gallant Poles never formally surrendered, the invaders had crushed resistance in just over a month.

Notwithstanding this breach of the understanding, the RAF meticulously observed the policy of not attacking civilian targets even to the extent of forbidding the bombing of enemy warships moored alongside in port for fear of killing civilian dockside workers.

Then on 14th May 1940 Germany launched a massive raid on Rotterdam which destroyed the historic centre of the city, killed 900 civilians and rendered 85,000 homeless. Germany had again broken the taboo about civilian targets and, moreover, warned that they would do the same to Utrecht if they did not receive the surrender of the Dutch Forces. To avoid massive loss of life and the destruction of more of its cities, the Dutch government sensibly, if reluctantly, surrendered and another European nation was under Nazi control.

With the destruction of Rotterdam, Germany had clearly declared that it was not prepared to have its military progress inhibited by the need to avoid civilian casualties. The gloves were off; Germany, with its greatly superior forces, intended to use the destruction of industrial targets to disrupt the Allied war effort and the levelling of civilian areas to undermine

Rotterdam City Centre after the German raid on 14th May 1940 which killed 900 civilians and rendered 85,000 homeless.

morale. Meanwhile, the huge German industrial areas of the Ruhr continued to pour out supplies of armaments to feed the voracious Nazi war establishment. Under these circumstances, it became no longer acceptable for Britain to unilaterally maintain the high principles of the unwritten concord which had clearly been abandoned by their enemy. On the night of 15th/16th May 1940, one day after the destruction of Rotterdam, Britain undertook its first aerial raid on factories in the Ruhr.

Britain's original aim had been for precision bombing of defined military, logistic and industrial targets but, by the end of the first year, had to accept that there was no such thing as precision bombing, a fact which was confirmed by the Butt Report in August 1941. As has been discussed earlier in this book, the RAF did not have the navigation technology to find their way to the targets and, even if these were positively identified, they did not have the bomb sights to ensure precision hits and every raid was liable to frustration by the unpredictable North European weather.

After the humiliation of its pathetically outnumbered and under-equipped expeditionary force at Dunkirk in May 1940, Britain had no chance whatever of engaging the enemy in mainland Europe until a citizen army had been recruited and weapons and equipment manufactured, or obtained, for their use. Undependable and largely ineffective as they were, Bomber Command's raids were the only means at Britain's disposal of aggressive action against the enemy in its homeland, and its occupied European territories, and this was to remain the case until the Normandy Landings in June 1944. British fighter aircraft were in continual action against enemy bombers but fighters were defenders; only bombers were attackers and their early efforts were vital to national morale. On 8th July 1941 Churchill emphasised their importance:

"There is one thing that will bring Hitler down and that is an absolutely devastating, exterminating attack by very heavy bombers from this country upon the Nazi homeland."

It was now recognized by Britain, as it had been by Germany since the start of the war, that anyone living in an industrial area must be regarded as being, either directly or indirectly, involved in support of the enemy war effort and, consequently, a legitimate target. It was never the primary objective of either side to attack civilians but an acceptance of the fact that civilian casualties were an inevitable consequence of strategic plans was now necessary.

Following Britain's first raid on Berlin on 28th August 1940, in response to Germany's bombing of London four days earlier (whether intentional or otherwise) there was a rapid escalation of bombing operations from both sides. In the 267 days between 7th September 1940 and 21st May 1941, the *Luftwaffe* mounted 124 major bombing raids on British cities which would later be known as 'The Blitz'. London suffered the worst with 71 separate attacks but major raids were also made on Liverpool, Manchester, Glasgow, Belfast, Sheffield, Hull, Birmingham, Coventry, Cardiff, Swansea, Bristol, Portsmouth, Southampton and Plymouth. More than 40,000 civilians were killed and possibly up to 100,000 injured. This was the first, full-scale, sustained use of area bombing by any nation. The previously mentioned response by Air Marshal Harris was characteristically robust:

> **"The Nazis entered this war under the rather childish delusion that they were going to bomb everybody else, and nobody was going to bomb them. At Rotterdam, London, Warsaw, and half a hundred other places, they put that rather naive theory into operation. They sowed the wind, and now, they are going to reap the whirlwind."**

Throughout the huge RAF raids on German cities which followed, continuous research and development was being undertaken to make navigation and bomb aiming more accurate, and therefore more selective, and great advances were made by the end of the war. In the meantime, the Germans who had invented 'Terror Bombing' now objected to its use against their own cities, a view which, as it became increasingly evident that the Allies were going to win, was beginning to be shared by liberal factions at home who could judge the moral issues from the comfort and safety of their own reserved occupations. In April 1942 a signal was received at the *Luftwaffe* High Command which set forth clearly Hitler's attitude to the 'terror' bombing of British cities:

> **The Führer has ordered that the air war against England be given a more aggressive stamp. Accordingly, when targets are being selected, preference is to be given to those where attacks are likely to have the greatest possible effect on civilian life. Besides raids on ports and industry, terror attacks of retaliatory nature are to be carried out against towns other than London. Minelaying is to be scaled down in favour of these attacks.**

Perhaps the best-known manifestation of the Germans' use of 'terror' was the siren fitted to their Ju87 *Stuka* dive-bombers the sole purpose of which was to strike fear into the hearts of their prey. Tens of thousands of civilian refugees from Poland, Belgium, the Netherlands and France would remember to their dying day the terrifying scream of the *Stukas* as they dropped out of the sky.

There is no doubt that many of the RAF bomber crewmen were uncomfortable with the civilian casualties their raids were creating but they were trained and disciplined airmen and did the job they were ordered to do to the best of their ability. After the war they were subjected from certain quarters to the same inane question which has so often been put to German soldiers: "Why did you not disobey an order which you considered to be illegal?" The answer is simple: military success, whether on land, air or sea, depends upon rigid discipline with commanders knowing that their soldiers, sailors or airman will do exactly what they are ordered to do when they are ordered to do it. It is not within the soldier's remit to decide whether or not an order is legal or morally acceptable. Junior ranks and rates do not question their orders. If every serviceman elected which orders he would obey and which he would ignore, the almost certain result would be his own death and that of many of his comrades. Any person who has served in the armed forces understands this and it is to our eternal shame as a nation that we should have allowed any sort of shadow to be cast over the achievements of the incredibly brave and dedicated men of Bomber Command.

The Royal Air Force was a young service desperately in need of a Battle Honour. Without in any way diminishing the bravery of the fighter pilots in the Battle of Britain, it is unfortunate that this comparatively insignificant campaign which lasted for less than four months should have been selected instead of the unremitting 'Battle of Germany', as it might well have been called, which was fought by Bomber Command for six long years. It is easy to understand: there was a certain glamour around debonair young heroes racing for their Spitfires and dicing with Messerschmitts in the blue summer skies over Kent; there was nothing romantic about bomber crews huddled in discomfort for hours on end, week after week, month after month, in the cold, vibrating fuselages of their aircraft as they clawed their way across the North Sea on their sacrificial missions deep into enemy territory. There can be little doubt that the men of Bomber Command earned a higher place in the honours and traditions of the Royal Air Force than their comrades in Fighter Command and the casualty figures for the whole war put their relative contributions into perspective:

	Fighter Command	Bomber Command
Killed	**3,690**	**55,573**
Wounded	**1,215**	**8,403**
Prisoners-of-War	**601**	**9,838**
Total casualties	**5,506**	**73,814**

There has also been much controversy over the effect of Bomber Command's activities upon enemy morale and industrial production. While Allied bombing never completely destroyed German morale, any more than the Blitz destroyed British morale, the effect on their production of war matériel was immense and the need to defend German cities from air attack required huge quantities of guns and ammunition, and thousands of soldiers to use them, who would otherwise be strengthening the ranks on the front lines. Albert Speer, Hitler's Minister of Armaments and War Production, considered that the Allied bombing offensive constituted Germany's greatest defeat. He wrote after the war:

Albert Speer, the German Minister of Production in 1933. Speer considered the Allied bombing offensive to have been Germany's greatest defeat.

"The real importance of the air war consisted in the fact that it opened a second front long before the invasion in Europe . . . . Defence against air attacks required the production of thousands of anti-aircraft guns, the stockpiling of tremendous quantities of ammunition all over the country, and holding in readiness hundreds of thousands of soldiers, who in addition had to stay in position by their guns, often totally inactive, for months at a time . . . . No one has yet seen that this was the greatest lost battle on the German side."

The achievements of Fighter Command, on the other hand, were less spectacular with their performance being completely eclipsed by that of other nations. The fighter pilots of the *Luftwaffe* were in a class of their own. Of the top 350 fighter aces of the Second World War, 333 were Luftwaffe pilots (6 were Soviet, 7 were Japanese, 1 was a Romanian and 3 were Finns). It may seem grotesque to rank pilots by their number of 'kills', but this is what war is all about and is the only way of comparing their achievements, if not always their ability. In this ranking, the top RAF fighter pilot, Marmaduke 'Pat' Pattle, a South African, would come in at No. 390 followed by James 'Johnnie' Johnson at No. 397. The top aces by nationality, shown opposite, may provide some surprises for those raised on the cordial mythology of the Battle of Britain.

It may also be noted that 107 *Luftwaffe* pilots had 100 or more victories and 45 German nightfighter pilots amassed kills of over 34 aircraft each, the total of Britain's top fighter ace. Throughout the war as tactics were steadily developed, the Allied bombers faced the most skilled and most successful fighter force of all time.

While invective flowed freely among civilians of both sides who were victims, or potential victims, of the 'Terror Bombing', there was a surprisingly restrained animosity between the RAF crews and their *Luftwaffe* adversaries, each side recognising in the other, men very similar to themselves, doing much the same job and motivated by the same feelings of patriotism and desire to defend their families and their homes. As with sailors and the sea, there was an unwritten camaraderie between airmen which in no way blunted their fighting zeal but often resulted in a touching magnanimity in victory. We have seen how Helmut Lent showed concern for his victims, entertained RAF survivors in his own officers' mess and visited wounded prisoners in hospital. There are also many cases on record of shot-down bomber crews being rescued by *Luftwaffe* personnel from lynch mobs of civilians crazed by the destruction of their towns and cities. There could be no love between the two sides but there was considerable admiration and respect.

It was Air Marshal Harris's contention that the war could be won by bombing alone and he stuck to his conviction until the end. One of the cornerstones of his argument was that the destruction of enemy cities, industry and transport would lessen the work needed to be done by Allied land forces thereby saving Allied lives. The same considerations applied later to the United States in deciding whether or not to drop the atomic bomb on Japan. The most controversial period of Bomber Command's activities was towards the end of the war in 1945 when Germany was effectively beaten, and the most contentious of the raids within this period was that undertaken by the RAF and USAAF against Dresden on 13th February.

TOP SCORING FIGHTER PILOTS WORLD WAR 2

Erich 'Bubi' Hartmann	top German (of all time)	352
Heinz-Wolfgang Schnaufer	top German (nightfighter)	121
Ilmari Juutilainen	top Finnish	94
Tetsuzo Iwamoto	top Japanese	80
Ivan Kozhedub	top Soviet and top Allied	62
Constantin Cantacuzino	top Romanian	56
Mato Dukovac	top Croatian	44
Richard Bong	top USAAF	40
Marmaduke 'Pat' Pattle	top South African (RAF)	40
James 'Johnnie' Johnson	top British	34
Pierre Clostermann	top Free French (RAF)	33
Brendan 'Paddy' Finucare	top Irish (RAF)	32
Ján Režák	top Slovak	32
George 'Buzz' Beurling	top Canadian (RAF)	31
Dezgö Szentgyörgyi	top Hungarian	30
Clive Caldwell	top Australian (RAF)	28
Colin Gray	top New Zealander (RAF)	27
Teresio Martinoli	top Italian	22
Stanislaw Skalski	top Polish (RAF)	19
Karel Kuttelwascher	top Czech (RAF)	18
John Plagis	top Rhodesian (RAF)	16
Stoyan Stoyanov	top Bulgarian	15
Liu Chi-Sheng	top Chinese (Nationalist)	11
Steve Pisanos	top Greek (RAF/USAAF)	10
Hugh Godefroy	top Dutch (RAF/RCAF)	7
William Anderson	top Swedish (USAAF)	7
Remy van Lierde	top Belgian (RAF)	6

It is often said by critics of the Allied attack on Dresden that there was no strategic reason for it at that stage of the war. This is not the case. At the Yalta Conference in the first week of February 1945 the Soviet delegation asked for the cooperation of Britain and America in heavy bombing of cities behind the German front lines on the Eastern Front. The strategic reasons for such raids would be the disruption of communications, resupply of the German forces and their eventual withdrawal; this would assist the Soviet advance on Berlin and thereby shorten the war. The cities identified as key positions in this strategy were Berlin, Dresden, Chemnitz and Leipzig and plans were consequently drawn up for a major Anglo-American offensive. The fact that US intelligence had identified several factories in Dresden producing war matériel while sheltering behind the immunity which the cultural heritage of the city had so far given them, was additional justification.

The raid on Dresden destroyed the major part of the city and caused a firestorm which resulted in massive casualties. It also justified its strategic aims of throwing enemy transport and communications networks into complete confusion to the benefit of the Russian advance. During several very heavy raids in March, Bomber Command dropped 67,637 tons of bombs on Germany, roughly the same as they had dropped in the first three years of the war. They had also perfected their techniques, as they had been paid and enjoined to do, in causing the maximum destruction of their targets. Now, having reached this peak of proficiency, they were to be castigated for the excellence they had for so long striven and had suffered so heavily to achieve.

Critics of the bomber offensive argue that this, and other raids which followed, were inhuman and unnecessary in strategic terms. But war is an inhuman business and its purpose is to kill as many of the enemy as possible while minimising casualties on one's own side. Germany was still fighting and killing Allied servicemen which justified to Harris his determination to continue with the destruction of German cities until the enemy stopped fighting and surrendered. There can be no doubt that many thousands of families in the British Commonwealth and the United States owe the safe return of fathers, brothers and sons to this policy. In a memo to the Air Ministry following the Dresden raid Harris wrote:

"Attacks on cities like any other act of war are intolerable unless they are strategically justified. But they are strategically justified in so far as they tend to shorten the war and preserve the lives of Allied soldiers. To my mind we have absolutely no right to give them up unless it is certain that they will not have this effect. I do not personally regard the whole of the remaining cities of Germany as worth the bones of one British Grenadier."

While "They did it first" is never an acceptable reason for doing the same, one must consider that in the early stages of the war Britain was in danger of being overwhelmed by a hugely powerful and evil regime against which citizens were exhorted to use every means available to them. Britain was unprepared militarily, her armed services grossly outnumbered and under equipped, and could not afford the luxury of liberal and humanitarian views against an enemy which had clearly rejected them.

As British citizens saw the news coverage of the wholesale destruction of European cities by the Nazis, the huge death toll among civilians and the ruthless attacks on women and children in refugee columns, they were ready to give their full support to any form of action against an enemy which was fighting dirty and would no doubt do the same in Britain if they were ever allowed to invade. At the time, any means would justify the end of defeating the Nazis and it was grossly ungenerous to condemn these attitudes from the stability of a victorious society enjoying the peace and freedom which were won by a commitment to destroy the enemy and not by moral and humanitarian aspirations; and it is still ungenerous today to disparage the actions of Bomber Command and to diminish the enormous contribution it made to Allied victory.

**Allan 'Jock' Richardson aged 20 in 1940 and aged 95 in 2015.
As a Wireless Operator/Air Gunner in No. 38 Squadron, Allan flew from
Marham on several of the same operations as Alec in 1940.**

Acknowledgements
and Principal Sources consulted

This was the story of my uncle, Alexander Ollar, whose medals, log book, correspondence, papers and photographs I inherited in 1998 and upon which this book is largely based. It is not a work of scholarship so I have not burdened the text with references and footnotes; readers must accept or dismiss the facts and statistics I have included as their experience or their fancy dictates.

I have never flown in a World War 2 bomber but have spoken at length with several who have, and have read the personal accounts of many more. I have tried, wherever possible, to contact those old airmen upon whose experiences of 75 years ago I have drawn so heavily in the reconstruction of this story. In almost all cases I have not been successful which is hardly surprising as those who are still alive are now mostly over 90 years of age. I am confident, however, that they would all have happily allowed me to borrow their experiences and emotions for any project which would strengthen public awareness of the achievements and sacrifices made by that branch of the armed services which has all-too-often been overlooked or regarded with uneasiness by historians.

In particular I would mention Sergeant (later Warrant Officer) Don Bruce a navigator in 115 Squadron, Marham from 25th May to 13th July 1942. He flew on some of the same operations as Alec and was shot down on 13th/14th July 1942. He spent the rest of the war as a POW and has left an excellent collection of his reminiscences on the internet including a detailed account of the raid in which Alec was lost. I have tried hard to contact his daughter without success.

In April 2015 I had the honour of meeting 95 year-old former Flight Lieutenant Allan (Jock) Richardson who, as a Wireless Operator/Air Gunner in 38 Squadron, Marham, knew Alec and flew on some of the same operations as him in 1940. He is identified in the photographs of the 38/115 Squadron crews who first bombed Berlin. Allan later trained as a pilot and served a full career in the RAF.

Much is available on the internet and other published sources about Helmut Lent but for the personal details of his life I have relied almost entirely on the late Peter Hinchcliffe's excellent book 'The Lent Papers' to which I readily direct anyone wishing for a more full account of the life and achievements of this remarkable German officer.

I hope readers will excuse the very poor quality of many of the photographs I have included. Many of them were taken by amateur photographers using the very basic, point-and-shoot 'Box Brownie' type of cameras which were in use by amateurs 70 years ago. I have worked on the assumption that enthusiasts would prefer a very poor picture to no picture at all.

Anyone who is interested in aviation history must be indebted to the small groups of volunteers, all over Europe but particularly in the 'Bomber Country' of Eastern England, who give up their time to collect exhibits and restore historic aircraft, airfield buildings and other wartime artefacts for the interest and enjoyment of future generations who may well find it difficult to believe the sheer scale of the World War 2 bomber offensive. There are many small, independently run, aircraft museums in the East of England. Of these I would mention, for example, the dedicated people who set up the "100th Bomb Group USAAF Memorial Museum" on the site of the former RAF Thorpe Abbotts, near Diss in Norfolk, one of the 41 airfields taken over by the Americans in 1943; we must never forget that they fought the bomber war alongside our own airmen for three years and their losses, also, were grievous. On the other side of the North Sea near Arnhem in Holland, the Deelen former *Luftwaffe* station from where Helmut Lent flew for much of his amazing career, is the site of a superb small museum run entirely by volunteers. It is in desperate need of funds in order to remain in existence and, as it does so much to honour the thousands of RAF crewmen who crashed in the Netherlands, it would be tragic if it had to close.

In April 2015, Group Captain H Smyth, Station Commander at RAF Marham, kindly consented to a visit by myself and two friends to the airfield from which Alec flew on both his operational tours. I am indebted to our guide during our tour of the station, Flight Lieutenant James Pettit RAF, to Mrs Andrea Dodds for coordinating our visit and to Warrant Officer

Steve Roberts, the Station Warrant Officer and Custodian of the Marham Heritage Centre which contains a splendid collection of records and other items of interest concerning RAF Marham, much of which has been collected and annotated by Steve who is a mine of knowledge and a true enthusiast. I shall shortly be donating Alec's DFM, logbook, photographs and other items to this collection.

I am also indebted to several friends and acquaintances for their support and assistance: Dr Adrian Pilling, a former RAF Medical Officer, who has been my fellow conspirator in this and other historical projects over the years; Squadron Leader (Retired) Adrian Richardson, son of Allan Richardson and himself a career RAF pilot who, among many other aircraft, flew Victor Tankers during the Falklands War; Rod and Anne Knight of Boscastle, a joint treasury of information on Air Force matters in general and North Cornwall in particular; Derrick Fawcett of the RAF Disclosures Branch for his assistance in tracing the records of service of several of Alec's fellow crewmen; Ronald Dunning for his usual help with research and genealogy; Anna Stone, the Aviva Group Archivist, for details of Alec's pre-war employment; Anthony Sheridan, a friend in Canada, for locating background information of the Kostyshyn family and to Ed Kostyshyn of Melville, Saskatchewan, for providing it; Michael Cousens of Buenos Aires for sending me a photograph of his father, Wing Commander Alan Cousens, and Iain Somerville of the Burntisland Heritage Trust for assistance with Alec's earlier life.

I am, as always, deeply grateful for the support and advice which I have received from Brigadier Henry Wilson, Publishing Manager of Pen & Sword, who has been my professional luminary for the past fifteen years and last, but certainly not least, my thanks to Natalie Gilbert, my friend and business partner of some 50 years standing, my greatest source of encouragement and my harshest and most valued critic.

Principal sources I have consulted in preparing this book are as follows:

Private Collection

The Flying Log Book, Papers, Photographs and Personal Correspondence of Pilot Officer A J S Ollar, DFM, RAFVR

National Archives

   AIR27/887, *115 Squadron Operations Record Books,*
      July-December 1940

   AIR27/889, *115 Squadron Operations Record Books,*
      May-July 1942

   AIR27/894-895, *115 Squadron Operations Record Books,*
      Appendices

   AIR50/213/13-18-1c, *115 Squadron Combat Reports* 1942

Air Ministry

   Pilots Notes for Wellington iii, x, xi xii and xiv,
      (reprinted by Crécy Publishing)

Aders, Gebhard

   History of the German Nightfighter Force 1917-1945
      Janes Publishing 1978

Becker, Cajus

   The Luftwaffe War Diaries, the German Air Force in World War II
      De Capo Press, New York, 1994

Bowman, Martin,

   RAF Bomber Command, Vol. 1 (Pen & Sword Aviation 2011)
   RAF Bomber Command, Vol. 2 (Pen & Sword Aviation 2012)
   The Wellington Bomber Story (The History Press, 2011)

Burt-Smith, Jim,

   Memoirs of a Goldfish (Woodfield Publishing 2000)

Bury, George,

   Wellingtons of 115 Squadron over Europe (Airforce
      Publishing Service 1994)

Hastings, Max,

   Bomber Command (Michael Joseph 1979)

Hinchcliffe, Peter,

   The Lent Papers (Cerberus Publishing 2003)

Longmate, Norman,

   The Bombers (Hutchinson 1983)

Middlebrook, Martin and Everitt, Chris,
  The Bomber Command War Diaries (Viking 1985)

Rivaz, R.C. Squadron Leader, DFC,
  Tail Gunner (Jarrolds 1943, Reprinted by The History Press 2011)

Saward, Dudley
  Bomber Harris, the Authorised Biography, Sphere 1988

Sawyer, Tom, Group Captain, DFC,
  Only Owls and Bloody Fools fly at Night (William Kimber 1982)

Smith, Ron, DFM,
  Rear Gunner Pathfinders (Goodall Publications 1987)

Webster, Sir Charles and Frankland, Noble,
  The Strategic Air Offensive against Germany 1939-1945
      Vol.i, (HMSO 1961)

Wilson, Kevin,
  Bomber Boys (Weidenfeld and Nicolson 2005)

Internet Sources

  Sergeant Don Bruce, 115 Squadron RAF, WWII
      www.darleys.pwp.blueyonder.co.uk/dad/

  Commonwealth War Graves Commission, www.cwgc.org

  Forces War Records, www.forces-war-records.co.uk

  Wikipedia, https://en.wikipedia.org
      115 Squadron RAF
      Helmut Lent
      List of World War II Flying Aces
      RAF Bomber Command
      RAF Marham
      Strategic Bombing
      The Blitz
      Vickers Wellington
      and many other subjects.

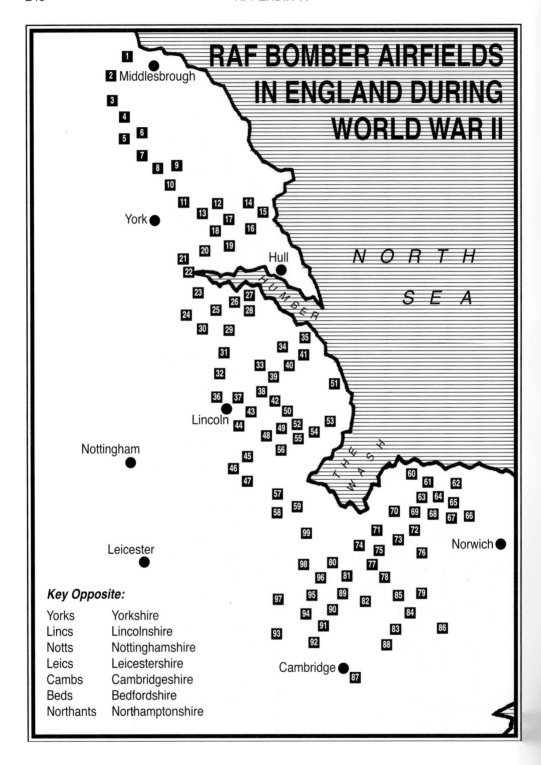

RAF BOMBER AIRFIELDS IN ENGLAND DURING WORLD WAR II

NORTH SEA

THE WASH

HUMBER

Middlesbrough
York
Hull
Nottingham
Lincoln
Leicester
Norwich
Cambridge

Key Opposite:

Yorks	Yorkshire
Lincs	Lincolnshire
Notts	Nottinghamshire
Leics	Leicestershire
Cambs	Cambridgeshire
Beds	Bedfordshire
Northants	Northamptonshire

1. Middleton St George, Durham
2. Croft, North Yorks
3. Leeming, North Yorks
4. Skipton-on-Swale, North Yorks
5. Dalton, North Yorks
6. Topcliffe, NorthYorks
7. Dishforth, North Yorks
8. Tholthorpe, North Yorks
9. East Moor, North Yorks
10. Linton-on-Ouse, North Yorks
11. Rufforth, North Yorks
12. Full Sutton, North Yorks
13. Elvington, North Yorks
14. Driffield, North Yorks
15. Lisset, North Humberside
16. Leconfield, North Yorks
17. Pocklington, North Yorks
18. Melbourne, North Yorks
19. Holme-on-Spalding-Moor, N Yorks
20. Breighton, North Yorks
21. Burn, North Yorks
22. Snaith, North Humberside
23. Lindholme, South Yorks
24. Finningley, South Yorks
25. Bottesford, Lincs
26. Elsham Wolds, Lincs
27. North Killingholme, Lincs
28. Kirmington, Lincs
29. Hemswell, Lincs
30. Blyton, Lincs
31. Ingham, Lincs
32. Scampton, Lincs
33. Faldingworth, Lincs
34. Binbrook, Lincs
35. Grimsby, Lincs
36. Wiggsley, Notts
37. Skellingthorpe, Lincs
38. Dunholme Lodge, Lincs
39. Wickenby, Lincs
40. Lindford Magna, Lincs
41. Kelstern, Lincs
42. Fisherton, Lincs
43. Waddington, Lincs
44. Swinderby, Lincs
45. Syerston, Notts
46. Newton, Notts
47. Langar, Notts
48. Balderton, Notts
49. Metheringham, Lincs
50. Bardney, Lincs
51. Strubby, Lincs
52. Woodhall Spa, Lincs
53. Spilsby, Lincs
54. East Kirby, Lincs
55. Coningsby, Lincs
56. Fulbeck, Lincs
57. Cottesmore, Lincs
58. North Luffenham, Leics
59. Woolfox Lodge, Lincs
60. North Creake, Norfolk
61. Little Shoring, Norfolk
62. Oulton, Norfolk
63. Sculthorpe, Norfolk
64. Foulsham, Norfolk
65. Swannington, Norfolk
66. Horsham St Faith, Norfolk
67. Attlebridge, Norfolk
68. Swanton Morley, Norfolk
69. West Raynham, Norfolk
70. Great Massingham, Norfolk
71. Marham, Norfolk
72. Watton, Norfolk
73. Bodney, Norfolk
74. Downham Market, Norfolk
75. Methwold, Norfolk
76. East Wretham, Norfolk
77. Feltwell, Norfolk
78. Lakenheath, Suffolk
79. Honington, Suffolk
80. Mepal, Cambs
81. Witchford, Cambs
82. Newmarket, Suffolk
83. Stradishall, Suffolk
84. Chedburgh, Suffolk
85. Tuddenham, Suffolk
86. Wattisham, Suffolk
87. Wratting Common, Cambs
88. Ridgewell, Essex
89. Waterbeach, Cambs
90. Oakington, Cambs
91. Bourn, Cambs
92. Gransden Lodge, Beds
93. Tempsford, Beds
94. Graveley, Cambs
95. Wyton, Cambs
96. Warboys, Cambs
97. Alconbury, Cambs
98. Upwood, Cambs
99. Polebrook, Northants

USAAF BOMBER AIRFIELDS IN ENGLAND DURING WORLD WAR II

1. Alconbury, Cambs
2. Andrew's Field, Essex
3. Attlebridge, Norfolk
4. Bassingbourn, Cambs
5. Birch, Essex
6. Bodney, Norfolk
7. Boreham, Essex
8. Bottisham, Cambs
9. Bovingdon, Herts
10. Boxted, Essex
11. Bungay, Suffolk
12. Bury St Edmunds, Suffolk
13. Chipping Ongar, Essex
14. Debach, Suffolk
15. Debden, Essex
16. Deopham Green, Norfolk
17. Duxford, Cambs
18. Earl's Colne, Essex
19. East Wretham, Norfolk
20. Eye, Suffolk
21. Fersfield, Norfolk
22. Fowlmere, Cambs
23. Framlingham, Suffolk
24. Glatton, Cambs
25. Gosfield, Essex
26. Great Ashfield, Suffolk
27. Great Dunmow, Essex
28. Halesworth, Suffolk
29. Hardwick, Norfolk
30. Hethel, Norfolk
31. Honington, Suffolk
32. Horham, Suffolk
33. Horsham St Faith, Norfolk
34. Kimbolton, Cambs
35. Knettishall, Suffolk
36. Lavenham, Suffolk
37. Leiston, Suffolk
38. Little Staughton, Cambs
39. Little Walden, Essex
40. Martrlesham Heath, Suffolk
41. Matching Green, Essex
42. Mendlesham, Suffolk
43. Metfield, Suffolk
44. Molesworth, Cambs
45. North Pickenham, Norfolk
46. Nuthampstead, Herts
47. Old Buckenham, Norfolk
48. Oulton, Norfolk
49. Podington, Beds
50. Rackheath, Norfolk
51. Rattlesden, Suffolk
52. Raydon, Suffolk
53. Ridgewell, Essex
54. Rivenhall, Essex
55. Sculthorpe, Norfolk
56. Seething, Norfolk
57. Shipdham, Norfolk
58. Snailwell, Cambs
59. Snetterton Heath, Norfolk
60. Stansted, Essex
61. Steeple Morden, Cambs
62. Sudbury, Suffolk
63. Thorpe Abbots, Norfolk
64. Thurleigh, Beds
65. Tibenham, Norfolk
66. Wattisham, Suffolk
67. Watton, Norfolk
68. Wendling, Norfolk
69. Wethersfield, Essex
70. Wittering, Cambs
71. Wormingford, Essex

Key:

Beds	Bedfordshire
Cambs	Cambridgeshire
Herts	Hertfordshire
Northants	Northamptonshire

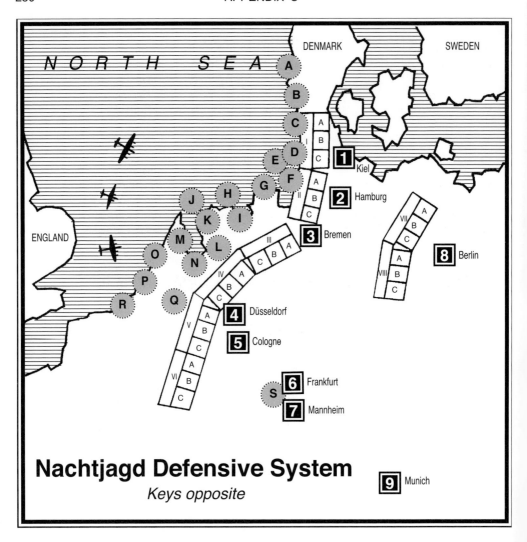

Nachtjagd Defensive System
Keys opposite

Dunkle Nachtjagd (DuNaJa) Areas
'Dark' Nightfighting Areas with radar-assisted interception without searchlights. Each area had *Freya* (long-range) and *Würzburg* (close control) radars and a beacon around which the nightfighters would circle while waiting for direction to a target.

Helle Nachtjagd (HeNaJa) Areas
'Light' Nightfighting Areas with radar-assisted interception in cooperation with searchlights for defence of the major cities.

The boxes with Roman numerals are the nightfighter *Räumes* or zones each subdivided into three sub-zones A, B and C.

DuNaJa Areas			F	Wal	M	Hering
			G	Jaguar	N	Hase
A	Büffel		H	Schlei	O	Zander
B	Robbe		I	Gazelle	P	Biber
C	Auster		J	Tiger	Q	Gorilla
D	Pelikan		K	Löwe	R	Hamster
E	Hummer		L	Marder	S	Kranich

HeNaJa Areas

			5	Cologne	Colibri
1	Kiel	Kiebitz	6	Frankfurt	Dachs-N
2	Hamburg	Hummel	7	Mannheim	Dachs-S
3	Bremen	Roland	8	Berlin	Bär
4.	Düsseldorf	Drossel	9	Munich	Mücke

Typical Structure of a Nachtjagdgeschwader
(Nightfighter Formation)

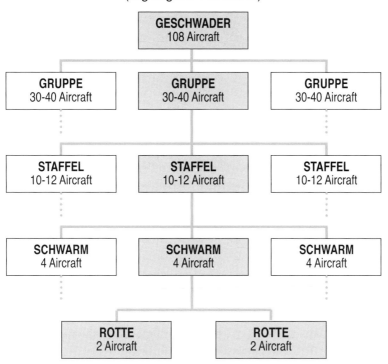

A *Staffel* was roughly equivalent to an RAF Squadron and the *Schwarm* to an RAF Flight.
The *Rotte* was the Luftwaffe's basic patrol formation of two aircraft.

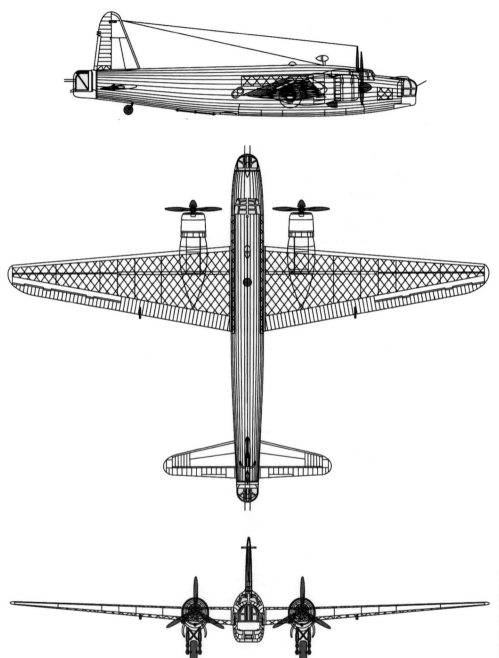

Vickers Wellington Mk III

Engines:	2 x Bristol Hercules III 14 cylinder, 2-row, radial engines 1,425 HP each

Length:	64.57 ft (19.68 m)
Wingspan:	86.15 ft (26.26 m)
Height:	16.40 ft (5 m)
Weight (empty)	18,971 lbs (8,605 kg)

Max speed:	261 mph (420 km/h)
Max Range:	1,540 miles (2,478 km)
Service Ceiling:	22,700 ft (6,919 m)

Armaments:	.303 ins (7.7 mm) Machine Guns 2 in Nose Turret 4 in Tail Turret 2 in Beam Positions

Total Produced:	11,461 (all versions)
In Production:	1936 - 1945
In Service:	1936 - 1953

Crew:	Pilot Co-Pilot Navigator Wireless Operator / Air Gunner Air Gunner (Air Gunner)

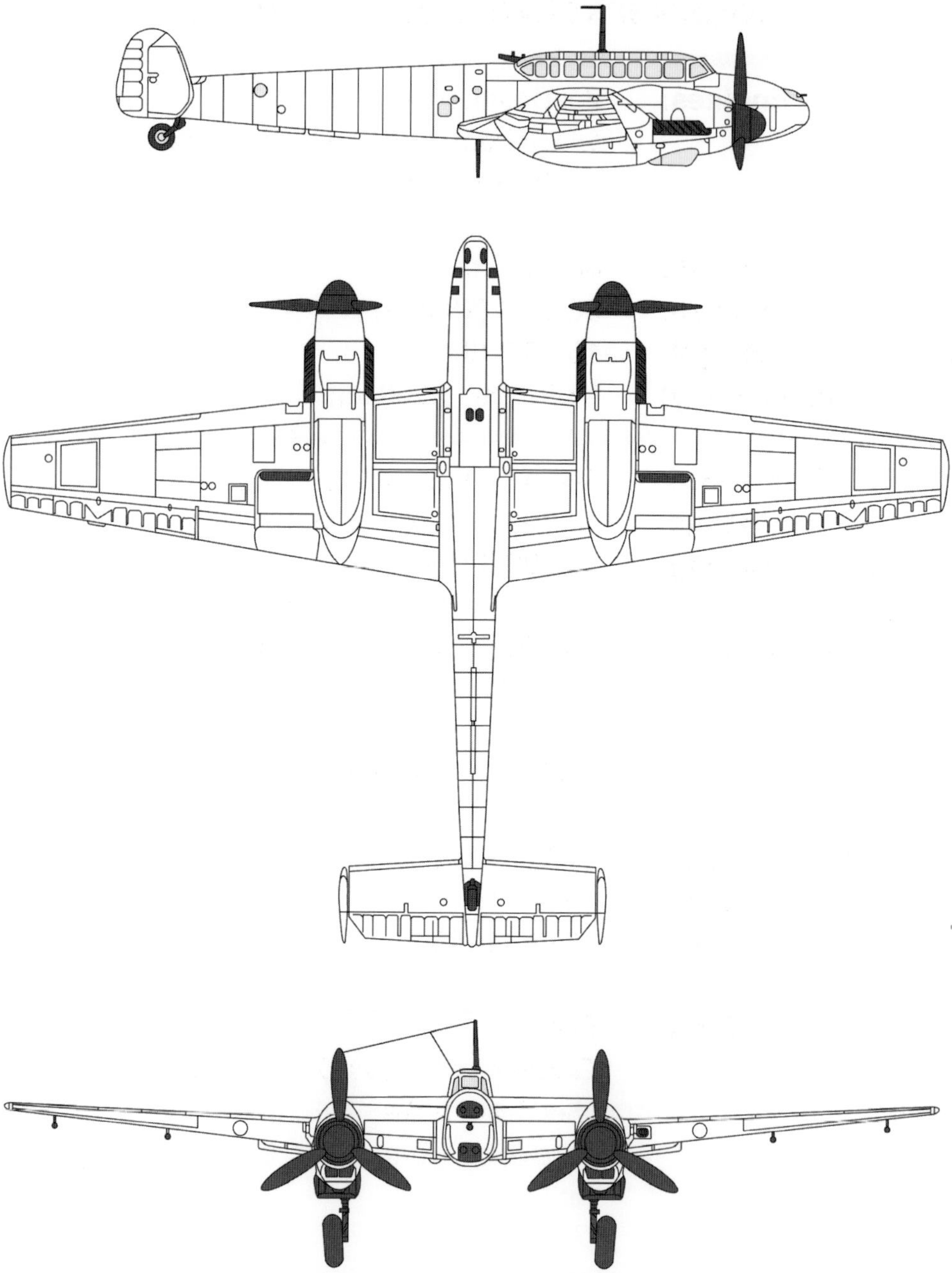

EVOLUTION GRAPHICS BV

Messerschmitt Bf 110 F

Engines:	2 x Daimler-Benz 601 B Liquid cooled, Inverted V-12 engines 1,085 HP each
Length:	40.5 ft (12.3 m)
Wingspan:	53.35 ft (16.3 m)
Height:	10.75 ft (3.3 m)
Weight (empty)	9,921 lbs (4,500 kg)
Max speed:	348 mph (560 km/h)
Max Range:	1,500 miles (2,410 km)
Service Ceiling:	35,000 ft (10,500 m)
Armaments:	2 x MG FF 20 mm cannon (.787 ins) 4 x MG17 7.92 mm (.312 ins) Front Facing Machine Guns 1 x MG15 Rear Facing Machine Gun
Total Produced:	6,170 (all versions)
In Production:	1936 - 1945
In Service:	1937 - 1945
Crew:	Pilot Gunner / Wireless Operator (*Funker*) (Second *Funker*)

Abbreviations

AG	Air Gunner
Air Cdre	Air Commodore
Air Chf Mshl	Air Chief Marshal
Air Mshl	Air Marshal
AVM	Air Vice Marshal
Bart	Baronet
Fg Off	Flying Officer
Flt Lt	Flight Lieutenant
Flt Sgt	Flight Sergeant
Gp Capt	Group Captain
Hants	Hampshire
HM	His/Her Majesty
HMS	His/Her Majesty's Ship
KRIEGS	Kriegsmarine (German Navy)
Leics	Leicestershire
Lt Col	Lieutenant Colonel
Maj Gen	Major General
Middx	Middlesex
MP	Member of Parliament
MRAF	Marshal of the Royal Air Force
Nav	Navigator
PF	Pathfinder
Plt	Pilot
Plt Off	Pilot Officer
RAAF	Royal Australian Air Force
RAFVR	Royal Air Force Volunteer Reserve
RCAF	Royal Canadian Air Force
RN	Royal Navy
RNZAF	Royal New Zealand Air Force
Sqn	Squadron
Sqn Ldr	Squadron Leader
TS	Turbine Steamer
USAAF	United States Army Air Force
Wg Cdr	Wing Commander
WO	Warrant Officer
W/Op	Wireless Operator / Air Gunner

Index